MW00354289

You're going to love this _____ of fascinating stories, wonderful humor, pathos and program insights into the life of a bush missionary doctor. You will gain a new understanding of missions; and when you turn the last page, you won't be the same.

David Stevens, M.D.
CEO of Christian Medical & Dental Association

* * * * *

If you ever need a reason to be thankful for your life of ease, if you ever need the inspiration to do good work, if you've ever thought you're too old or inexperienced to do something dramatic and adventurous, then "Happiness Is A Fat Gecko" is the book for you. In this great collection of stories from the world of missionary medicine, long time emergency physician and medical educator, Dr. Frank Black, does a delightful job of inspiring, teaching and entertaining the reader with many short, digestible (and wonderfully honest) tales of the years he spent with his wife Lou Ann as they served the poor, sick and dying in Tanzania. Frank's career as a physician in the United States gives him a unique viewpoint with which to view life in rural Africa, where medicine is practiced with almost none of the resources we take for granted at even the poorest US hospital.

Physicians spend their lives accumulating stories. Here, Frank has given us (and his former patients in Tanzania), a wonderful gift by sharing them so that they can go on and on for years to come. So read this book and learn some Swahili, some self-examination, some geography, history, medicine, biology, and more.

And best of all, learn to keep things in perspective. After all, you have food, clean water, a nice car and air conditioning. And you don't need a fat Gecko to get by.

Edwin Leap, MD, FACEP
Emergency Physician and Medical columnist and blogger

Happiness is a Fat Gecko
Life and Times of a Missionary Doctor

Frank Black, M.D.

First published by Dog Ear Publishing
4011 Vincennes Rd
Indianapolis, IN 46268
www.dogearpublishing.net

ISBN: 978-1-4575-5951-8

This book is printed on acid-free paper.

Printed in the United States of America

DEDICATION

This book (my labor of love) is dedicated to the
love of my life (my wife, Lou Ann).
She was my stalwart companion
and willing co-worker on the mission field.
She continually showed me the way to love
and serve the people.

TABLE OF CONTENTS

(CHAPTERS)

INTRODUCTION

There I was at age 50 in July 1992 when my wife, Lou Ann, and I embarked on our missionary medicine odyssey. We moved to Chimala, Tanzania, where we committed to serve for five years at the Mission Hospital. Why now? Our youngest child of three had been out of college for a year and was gainfully employed. We had been blessed to work and save while working for nineteen years in Emergency Medicine in Indianapolis, Indiana. We had tremendous support for our endeavor, both emotionally and financially. Throughout my career in Emergency Medicine I had been looking for ways to use my medicine and my Christianity together more effectively. Now was the time. We now had no particular constraints in proceeding where prayers had led us. What we called our "Five Year Plan" in 1988 came to fruition in four years. This was due to many blessed events and the generosity of our church, friends, and organizations.

Over a period of several years Lou Ann and I had served in a number of developing countries on short-term medical mission trips. We now wanted to live and work long-term where there was tremendous medical need. Of the places we had been, Africa and the African people had stolen our hearts. Let me explain. My first trip abroad was in 1977 to Nigeria with Dr. Henry Farrar (this is the only trip I took without Lou Ann). Dr. Farrar had served in Nigeria for many years and was the founder of Nigerian Christian Hospital. I worked alongside him for a month. He was well known and loved, a fine Christian man, very experienced in the culture and tropical medicine, and a fine surgeon. What better introduction could I possibly have had! When I returned to Indianapolis, I told Lou Ann that she must go with me next time. Our love affair with medical missions and Africans had begun. I had found the way to serve — using my medicine and religion together where they were most needed.

I must tell you more about the African people. Their lives are very hard, and this is an understatement. Despite their hardships and limiting situations, they always maintain a rigorous work ethic and positive spirits. Their hardiness — their plain old toughness — is nothing short of amazing. Their patience and perseverance defy our imagination. Their lives are replete with much suffering and death; and yet they maintain a strong sense of family, community, and a joy — yes a joy. See why we fell in love with the Africans and wanted to help as best we could.

I had been trained and certified in Internal Medicine, but while in the Navy I made the decision to change to the new specialty of Emergency Medicine. Because of my medical work I had always been 'hospital-based.' Consequently, I thought that I could do more good medically in the developing world in the hospital setting. This is why I only looked at hospitals and ones sponsored by our fellowship (Church of Christ). After our survey trip in 1990 through four African countries, we chose Tanzania and Chimala Mission Hospital. The weather and living situation at Chimala were more suitable for us. Another reason we chose Tanzania was the language (Kiswahili). I'll just call it Swahili. It is the national language and is what I call "learnable". This is because unlike the tonal language of Nigeria, Swahili is a phonetic language. This makes it more learnable for one fifty year old poor language learner (me). The thought of always using a translator was simply out of the question. Being impatient by nature, coupled with my rapid fire ER approach to medicine, I just had to be able to speak the native language. (More about Swahili in a later chapter). I also considered the hospital 'manageable' compared to others I'd seen. This assessment later came to haunt me as you will see.

Having worked short-term in a Third World hospital several times, I was still unprepared for possibly being the only doctor in a hospital setting. My Emergency Medicine and Internal Medicine backgrounds prepared me well in many areas but left some deficits. The obvious areas were tropical medicine, obstetrics, and surgery. I had delivered babies as in Intern — some twenty-five years before but always with supervision. Likewise, I hadn't 'scrubbed in' for surgery since my Internship. I was able to 'scrub in' with some of my surgeon friends in order to learn a few procedures. Studying extensively by using textbooks and articles also helped mightily to supplement. These became my 'medical bible', if you will, when I found myself on the scene in Chimala. But you can see that my preparation left a lot to gumption, prayer, and plain old OJT (On the Job Training). More on this in ensuing chapters.

Why did it take me so long to write? I'm really not sure. I always thought I had some experiences and thoughts worthy of sharing and perhaps even something novel. I had kept fairly complete log books and these, together with my monthly newsletter entitled "Perspectives", supplied plenty of material. (At times I quote directly from the newsletter — this will be so noted). I wrote here and there in a piecemeal style for about a decade. As I think about it, there were several reasons for my procrastination. One is that most people think their life is worthy of a book. I didn't want to fall into that audacious category. Our experiences meant so much to Lou Ann and me I just didn't think my writing could do it justice. I didn't want to write just another book. Then there are the factors of time, incentive, and the obscure writer's block. For these reasons and more I just didn't have the urgency to finish. But despite it all, I'm now finished.

My book is not autobiographical. Perhaps it's more like my memoirs. It contains medical stories of course but extends beyond this into non-medical cultural observations and experiences. I always thought in terms of contrasts between our beloved Third World and the First World of our homeland. This is always done in a non-judgmental way, and I never intend to belittle or castigate — certainly with no thought of feeling superior. Simple observations readily depict the never ending diverse and drastic contrasts between the two worlds. Likewise the medical and cultural aspects vary from humorous to sad; from success to failure; from known to unknown; from good to bad; from healing to death. Janice Bingham's term, "bittersweet", sums up the overall feeling quite well.

When I went through my journals while writing, I would become transcended — feeling like I was right there in Chimala again. The same feelings, location, smells, and people are right there. It became quite an emotional experience. Simply stated, my book is about the life and times, experiences, and perspectives of a Third World missionary doctor.

The style of writing is that which I used in my Newsletters. It's not 'medical lingo'. For the most part I write in my own personal, casual style and for a wide range of people. When I get too technical, I try to offer an explanation. The chapters are a seeming collage of disjointed topics; but put together they paint a picture of the diversity of living, working, and serving in a Third World bush hospital. Let's together begin our Adventure in Missions.

Addendum:

- "Third World":
  You notice I most commonly use this term. It is probably not the latest "in phrase" to describe more underdeveloped countries, but you know the term. References speak of the "Developing World" or Two-Thirds World." I always hasten to clarify that the term is definitely not one intended to belittle or "put down" — not a term denoting inferiority. It is not a reflection of the people. It reflects a country's educational system, infrastructure, medicine, transportation, utilities, and so forth. These are the very reasons we want to help as much as possible. We are definitely needed more there. If I walked out of the American ER where I worked, I could be replaced the next day. If I did this in Tanzania, it would not be possible. (I refer to this aspect in the chapter, "Reflections.")
  I pursued the question, "What is Third World?", during our five years in Tanzania. The various chapters depict stories and situations that together help define the question. A follow-up question you might have is, "Why Does Third World Stay That Way?"

I'm sure this topic has been the subject of numerous PhD dissertations. I'll not attempt to explore this question.

- "Bush Hospital":

  I refer to our beloved Chimala Mission Hospital as a "bush hospital". You may wonder what I'm talking about. First of all Chimala is a small village and far removed from more advanced medical care. We were quite limited by the standards you know in the USA — even in very small hospitals. The following list will quickly amaze you with our limitations: (a partial list)
  - No cardiac or other monitoring systems
  - No neonatal incubator
  - Oxygen in tanks only (enough for 1-2 patients)
  - No automatic beds (military barracks-type beds and a few old hand crank beds)
  - No ultrasound machine
  - No EKG machine
  - No CT or MRI (Are you kidding!)
  - X-ray machine: We had what I called a "World War II" model machine that would do chest, abdomen, and bone films of fair quality at best.
  - Lab: No sodium, potassium, blood sugar, liver or kidney functions — and the list goes on and on. Imagine trying to care for a diabetic in acidosis or kidney failure without these. We did have the initial screening test for HIV/AIDS which was most valuable.

But lest you be dismayed and wonder what good we did for anyone, let me assure you that we took care of most patients quite effectively. After reading the book, see what you think.

"HAPPINESS IS A FAT GECKO"

*"The only ones among you who will be really happy
are those who will have sought and found how to serve."*

—Albert Schweitzer

O kay, let's get it out of the way right off the bat. Why the book title? For one reason perhaps it piques your interest. But it also sets the stage a bit humorously for a period of service and wonderment in our lives. Such an unusual title does deserve, however, an explanation. Over recent years you've seen a number of writings or sayings that begin with, "Happiness is _____". I always thought this was rather catchy, so I followed suit.

An all too common scurrying sound was frequently heard emanating from the walls and ceiling of our house on the Chimala compound. As we found out soon enough, some were good sounds and the others; oh well, I'll get to those later. With our love of art we had numerous pictures hanging in our otherwise drab but functional home. It seems that these pictures served as convenient 'rest stops' for our critters, as we called them. After our initial phase of being startled every time our geckos decided to change location, we came to appreciate our little buddies. You see; we came to know that they were part of our 'preventive medicine'. They accomplished this by feasting on those infernal malaria carrying mosquitoes and poisonous spiders. Our house, despite having "mosquito proof" screens, was all too well endowed with these buggers. Just let a mosquito land; and they would be in immediate, unexpected peril at the 'hands' of our now beloved geckos.

Over time we noticed that our geckos continued to grow and grow — into what we fondly called 'gecko obesity'. Thus the title, "Happiness Is A Fat Gecko." They were happy and contented and so were we. Of course all this was made possible because of the seemingly endless supply of 'food' that our house offered. I'm pretty sure we had the same geckos for our five years in the house. We even recognized some of them and gave them names: Henry, George, Sally, etc.

Our little buddies offered us another side benefit. Entertainment. This was the amusement they provided every time we had ex-patriot visitors from the USA. We purposely wouldn't warn our guests about the sudden rapid blur of motion and accompanying sound, as they changed location or dashed to ingest another meal. The resultant expected startle or shriek was inevitable. Only then would we clue in our guests.

Over time we became inured to them, and they were just part of our 'normal' house.

While I'm writing about *"Happiness Is _____"* situations, I'll include some others. These aren't particularly funny but would come under the realm of "doctor humor". Most of them have to do with times or events that would give a weary doctor a boost — an unexpected 'high' because things were going more smoothly — at least for now.

- So many times at Chimala I would be summoned with the all too familiar, *"shida OB"*. ('Shida' in Swahili means <u>problem</u>). Regarding OB, it's best to never wait when so summoned; consequently, I would drop whatever I was doing and dash to OB. Of course Murphy's Law is usually in effect, and the call to OB seemed to be inordinately at night. Experience had taught me that our staff tended to under estimate problems and often waited too long to call me. But occasionally, only occasionally, I would get to OB and hear the 'happy words'. Happiness is hearing: <u>*"She delivered doctor, and everything is fine."*</u> Joy fills my heart!

- What's the dread of all surgeons everywhere? I'll tell you; it's post-operative complications. They're very disheartening. So, <u>*"Happiness is the absence of post-operative complications."*</u> We went through times when many post-operative infections would occur. These are dangerous for the patient, time consuming, expensive, and use up many of our somewhat limited supply of medicines. At such times I would go through the entire surgical process in order to find any possible source of infection: cleaning and sterilization of instruments, towels, gauze, sheets, surgical gowns, the surgical room itself (more about this), the 'scrubbing' process of ourselves and the patients' operative site, etc. Speaking of the 'clean' surgical room (we had only one), it was virtually impossible to have any semblance of cleanliness. Let me see.......... too much people traffic, various assortment of insects that found their way in, the ubiquitous geckos, an occasional rat, outside air being sucked in through the occasionally functional air conditioner. Get the picture. Usually we could not pinpoint a specific cause for a higher infection rate; but after trying to remedy all we could, the infection rate would decline.

- Back to OB: _"Happiness is an empty Labor Room."_

- _"Happiness is NO burn cases."_ I absolutely hate burn cases — yes, hate. I'll have more to say about these cases later.

- _"Happiness is NO pediatric IV's to do."_ Yes, I can do them; but they are often quite difficult. Add their small size to the inevitable screaming and wiggling and you get the idea. Besides, we had Janice (our American Pediatric Nurse Practitioner), who could start an IV on a turnip. I knew if she couldn't start one, I was in real trouble. I hasten to add that IV's on small children were often absolutely vital and life saving. Even a very few minutes are critical in a severely dehydrated child.

- _"Happiness is a meningitis or cerebral malaria patient who awakens and is eating and talking."_ The type of malaria most common in East Africa is falciparum malaria. This type especially affects the brain (cerebral malaria) and can cause seizures, coma, and death. Bacterial meningitis (especially meningococcal meningitis) is the worst type of meningitis and is almost uniformly fatal without prompt antibiotic treatment. We had several outbreaks of meningococcal meningitis. The patient's ultimate outcome was almost totally dependent on how soon they came for treatment. A delayed presentation meant disaster — either permanent severe mental disability or death. Another added danger is that both cerebral malaria and meningitis can almost exactly mimic one another. This makes a spinal tap necessary to distinguish the two. And just to keep us on our toes, some patients had both.

- This goes without saying: *"Happiness is going through the night without being called!"* Boy, how rare this was! When I was on call, my last thought before going to sleep was a prayer to be able to respond quickly and appropriately when called — and to be nice. I do awaken quickly, but I'd be the first to admit that I have trouble being nice at times. And besides this, I forgot almost all my Swahili at night. Just ask Lou Ann or the Tanzanian staff — on second thought, don't.

- *"Happiness is the electricity being on."* This was never more true than when we had an emergency surgical case at night. More than once the National Power would be off and the hospital generator would be quite delayed or just ceased functioning. So what to do? The patient may be in shock and bleeding profusely or the unborn baby may be in severe distress, necessitating and immediate Caesarean section. One of my solutions was my trusty D-cell Maglite that always accompanied me to surgery at night. If all power was off or if the National Power went off during surgery and before the generator could be "cranked up", I would assign one person to be my "surgical light" holder. This is obviously far from the ideal, but it can be used — and successfully. There are several mothers and their children in Chimala who can attest to this fact. (Most of our night surgeries were Caesarean sections.)

LANGUAGE SCHOOL
AND LANGUAGE SNAFUS

*"The missionary work we do is a grain of sand;
the work untouched is an entire seashore."*

—Amy Carmichael

The national language of Tanzania is properly called Kiswahili. I'm calling it just Swahili as most of you know it. It was developed as a trade language and is based on the native Bantu languages of Eastern Africa in addition to Portuguese and Arabic. Our first four months in Tanzania were spent at the Lutheran Seminary in Morogoro, Tanzania, attending language school. Remember that one of our reasons for choosing to serve in Tanzania was that the language was "learnable". Wow, did that remain to be seen. At least I had the good sense to go to language school first and before beginning to work at the hospital. The hospital was in dire need of another physician and would have basically encompassed all my time. Fortunately I resisted the advice of many on our compound who said, "Oh, you can learn it here at the hospital." This would absolutely NOT have been possible.

There were about sixty-five students in our class from many countries — USA, England, Ireland, Germany, Italy, Poland, Czechoslovakia, Lichtenstein,, Singapore, and a few countries I've forgotten. I was never a good "language learner", and being fifty years old didn't help matters any. I had long since lost what abilities I had in this area. My only saving grace was that the course was taught in English, even though our main teacher was from Sweden. Her English was what she called "proper British English".

We had class five days a week and about seven hours a day. This included drill sessions (I called them 'grill sessions'). I can truthfully say that I've not studied as hard at anything since medical school. Lou Ann will definitely vouch for me. Frankly, I drove her nuts.

Before I go further, let me tell you some things about our school. We stayed in one small room much like a dorm room. It opened to an outside corridor. There were no amenities in the room, and the bathroom and shower were down the outside corridor. I should tell you that we had no hot water. Our four months there approached the hotter months, and I never ever got used to cold showers. Did I say I never got used to them? In fact, I got so tired of them that I bought the largest plastic tub I could find in the market — one I could sit in. Then I bought the largest metal coil, so I could heat the water. This of course was predicated upon the electricity being on. True to Murphy's Law, this became more and more infrequent. About once per week I'd fill the tub about half full, immerse the coil, plug it in until the water was piping hot, and just sit there — while studying. While writing about bathroom functions, I'll tell you our toilet paper was non-absorbent and doubled as crape paper — very 'stretchy'.

And then there's the food. Or I should say the lack of food. Since there were quite a number in our class, plus some small children; we had to eat in two shifts. The cafeteria would not accommodate everyone simultaneously. The families with small children went first and us oldies next. You got it; there would often be very little left for us to eat — especially meat. Add this to the fact that we had no vending machines and no food market nearby. As a result, yours truly was hungry most of the time. I didn't need to lose weight but began to melt away. We just had to do something. Protein was needed big time. We found a German butcher in Morogoro and purchased some sausages and secured some peanut butter from our Chimala compound. And oh yes, I must not forget the cheese. We learned from a classmate about a Catholic seminary that made and sold cheese. We had him buy us some. I don't know what kind it was but wow, did it ever stink. In fact, it was so bad that I hung it in a bag from the outside corridor's beams. I should say that its one of those cheeses that smells really bad but tastes kind of okay. Anyway, I ate it. In telling folks the "cheese story" I've embellished it by saying it smelled so bad that as a side benefit, it kept the mosquitoes away.

At times I felt like Abe Lincoln. Why? Because we had to study by candle light too often. I've mentioned our too frequent lack of electricity. We'd study as long as we could stand the bugs that the candles inevitably attracted. It was too dangerous to use the candles in bed with the mosquito net. Thinking about the possibility of fire, one evening we saw a fire in a room across the way. One of the students had left a burning candle near the window. With the wind whipping the curtains around, they caught fire. We rushed to help put it out, for the couple was not in their room. No significant damage was done — except to the curtains of course.

The basic rules of Swahili are fairly simple and straight forward, much like Spanish. Being a phonetic language means that there are basic, distinct sounds for each letter that don't depend on intonation or pitch. In Swahili the major vowels (A, E, I, O, U) have one and only one sound. Compare this to the multiple sounds of each vowel in English. Each major vowel used makes a separate syllable, and the accent is virtually always on the next to last syllable. There are very few exceptions — again so much unlike English. Now add that Swahili has no gender forms and no articles. Got it? This has been your Swahili grammar lesson.

Whether it was my age or simply my poor language learning skills, I struggled mightily. Once again, this was absolutely not for lack of study. With study I was able to learn the vocabulary words, the grammar, the parts of speech, and how to construct sentences to the nth degree — on paper. One problem! I had trouble 'hearing' the language. Now what does this mean? It means that something happened between my ears. I had to hear the words and sentences, let it assimilate in my brain, and then translate it into English before understanding what was said in Swahili. This is definitely not the way to learn a language. By the time my brain performed these functions, I was already two sentences behind. Just think how a small child learns a language. They learn by hearing it and then trying to say it over and over. They don't know the alphabet much less how to read. I had it exactly backwards! I was trying to read first and then hear and understand.

How poor a student was I, you ask? I kept getting demoted in our drill (or "grill") sessions until I was with the poorest group. What a lesson in humility this was for a physician who had passed all his Board Exams and been the Director of an Emergency Residency! I must admit this did bother me a bit. But my main objective was to be able to function in Swahili. So I was not deterred from my efforts and kept mightily plugging away. I called it the "BF" technique — that stands for "brute force."

The poorest group was composed of a couple teenaged boys whose parents were in the class. They weren't trying and really didn't care about learning the language. It was a joke to them. After only one session with them and their clowning around, I went to the director. I told her that I may be a poor language learner, but that I was trying very hard and could not put up with that group. Without further ado, she moved me to another group.

I'll give you an example of how you have to totally memorize Swahili vocabulary words. There are not many words that give you any hint of their meaning because of a similarity to English or other Latin based language. For example, the Swahili word for our simple word "wheel" is "*maguurudumu*". See what I mean. I do love the language of Swahili, but it is somewhat limited in terms of vocabulary. Consequently, it 'steals' words from other languages — especially English. This does result in making some of the words easy. For example: *betri* for battery; *waya* for wire; *jeki* for jack; *spea* for spare; *nati* for nut; etc. You can also readily see that in Swahili they don't like one syllable words or ones that end with a consonant. This made it difficult for the Tanzanians to call me Black. So it most frequently came out "Blacki" (two syllables ending with the vowel sound of "i").

It became all too commonplace for me to be close to the right word or pronunciation. I'd be close, but I'd be 'one letter off'. Lou Ann and Janice said they were going to put that on my tombstone — "*One Letter Off*". Lou Ann was much better than I was with language and had the habit of correcting me. If I made a mistake around her, I'd almost immediately hear this soft sound (like an echo) with the corrected word or statement. I'd be lying if I didn't tell you that this became rather annoying to me. Don't get me wrong; I was pleased that she did so well, but the ego or whatever in me resented the correction. I'm quite sure I made numerous severe and repeated errors in Swahili that never were brought to my attention. The Tanzanians were most gracious in their understanding and tolerance of me — and probably knew what I meant to say. They never corrected me unless I asked them.

One Saturday as we were driving to town with Janice and one of our language teachers, Janice thought she would use some of her newly acquired language. She said, "*Mimi ninaharibu Swahili kwa bidii.*" Basically she had said that she was trying to destroy Swahili. What she meant to say was, "*Mimi nianjaribu Swahili kwa bidii.*" This says she was trying very hard in Swahili, The root words are "*haribu*" meaning to destroy and "*jaribu*" meaning to try. Very close aren't they? One letter off.

Later Snafus and Misunderstanding:

Here's a good one: Once when I was telling someone of my conversation on the telephone, it came out drastically wrong. The Swahili word for telephone is "*simu*", and the word for poison is "sumu". Okay, you see what I did! I told them I was talking on the poison.

During a Bible lesson in chapel one morning, I made an unfortunate mistake. A man named Aliye had been hit and killed on the roadway in front of the hospital the previous evening. Aliye was somewhat mentally deficient and volunteered for odd jobs around the hospital. He was quite friendly and everyone knew him. I said, *"Aliye amekufa kesho."* I had said that, "Aliye has died tomorrow (*kesho* means tomorrow) I should have used the work *"jana"* instead — which means yesterday.

On one occasion when we had just returned from our likizo (furlough or leave), I was explaining our trip to the church assembly. My major snafu was using a word very close in spelling but quite different in meaning. In my "excellent Swahili" (ha!) I proceeded to tell them that, "We <u>walked</u> to America". I meant to say that, "We <u>visited</u> America". The verb for "to walk" is *"kutembea"* and the verb for "to visit" is *"kutembelea"*. See what I mean. Give me a break now; you'd probably do the same thing. Anyway, after a host of chuckles and being told what I said wrong, I corrected myself.

But the favorite snafu I'll tell on myself happened in the middle of the night just before surgery. Almost all the surgeries I did at night were Caesarean sections for babies or mothers in distress. I had a standard prayer I would say before each operation. It went something like this: *"Tunakushukuru Mungu kwa baraka zote na Mama huyu na mtoto yake......"* This says, "Thank you God for all blessings and for this mother and her baby....." Before the upcoming surgery I got this far in my stock prayer; then I stopped abruptly and couldn't hold back my snickers. You see; this 'woman' was really a man with an incarcerated hernia. The surgery crew couldn't hold back their laughter. I quickly started over and prayed for the MAN. In my defense I blame this snafu mostly on my fatigue, plus what I've said about my usual night time surgeries. (There's really no excuse.)

I eventually achieved a "functional" use of Swahili. I was far, far removed from fluency. Since I used 'medical Swahili' all the time, I did become quite proficient in this realm. I could ask someone in my sleep if they'd ever had fever or diarrhea, etc. Despite our limited abilities in the language, these meager attempts were always most appreciated by the Tanzanians. They were most understanding and forgiving of my snafus

— which I'm sure were too numerous to count. Of course you can add my slightly Southern Hoosier accent in with my too often snafus.

"The Rib Story":

One of our nurses raised pigs in order to make money on the side. Since most of the beef we purchased wasn't fit to eat, some of our best meat was Rainer's pigs — in addition to the *"wanyama wa porini"* (wild game that we occasionally had — impala, river buck, wildebeest, topi, etc.). Rainer also butchered the pigs for us, and Lou Ann very carefully told him how to prepare the ribs. We were really looking forward to bar-bequed ribs. When she went to pick up the meat, she said, "Where are the ribs?" "Oh, here they are Mama Blacki," as he proudly held up a small bag. It seems that something was once again lost in translation. Rainer had very carefully cut all the meat off the ribs and placed it in the bag. I think Lou Ann was able to contain herself as she thanked him — even though she was howling inside.

"Come; come; Mama Blacki's car has been attacked!":

This was the message that came to our house one evening. At the time I was indisposed with a long leg cast from my surgically repaired torn Achilles tendon. The message went to Bob Stapleton, our Mission Administrator. Bob didn't know whether to take his gun or what. Our area had recently been plagued by robberies, especially directed against missionary compounds. As it turned out, Bob rode his bicycle to the scene — minus his gun. What had happened was that our Toyota Land Cruiser was stuck in the mud, and Lou Ann couldn't get it out. In Swahili the word *"stuck"* when translated to English is like our word for *"attacked"*. Therefore to the Tanzanian relaying the message, the vehicle was "attacked by mud" or just "attacked" for short. Humorous, yes: but you can see that drastic miscues can and do occur. By the way, Lou Ann had forgotten to "lock in" the hubs on the front wheels. Uh oh. In that model it had to be done outside the vehicle on the wheel itself. Bob locked the hubs and easily drove out, thus taking care of the "attacked" vehicle.

"Black's House":

When we first moved to Chimala, our house was all prepared for us. This was complete with a large wooden placard mounted by the front door, simply saying, *"Black's House"*. Maybe you're ahead of me, but our sign grew to be an area of confusion. We had too many Tanzanians who couldn't find our house. "Why", you might ask. They thought the sign meant that this house was designated for those of a 'darker complexion'. We took the sign down.

Sweating in the Operating Room:

Swahili speakers often made up their own words, combining an English word with Swahili prefixes or suffixes. An example would be: *"amesweat"*. 'Sweat' is not a Swahili word, but *"ame..."* is added to the English word 'sweat'. The combination would mean 'he/she is sweating'. The proper Swahili way to express this would be, *"ametoka jasho"*. This basically says, "sweat is coming out of him/her". By the way, I first heard this expression from one of our surgical technicians. It was most apropos because sweat flowed most freely during the hot season especially during day surgeries. (Our A/C was either "imeharibika" (broken) or ineffective.). If you add the tropical climate, the skylight, the ineffective A/C, the surgical gowns, caps, masks, boots, and gloves; the result was a proverbial inferno. Sweat would pour down my face and onto my glasses. I always had a designated 'sweat wiper' for my forehead, glasses, and face. Sweat would run down my arms and fill up my surgical gloves. And yes, sometimes the 'sweat wiper' would be a bit late and sweat would drip into the operative field. Oops. No, sweat is not sterile. This was just another operative hazard among many others. Fortunately,

God's healing took over and rectified these and other situations. In preparation for such surgeries with its expected fluid loss I would pre-load with fluids, just like before a vigorous ball game or tennis match.

Remove the Weeds:

Lou Ann became quite the horticulturalist. We had beautiful flowers around our house that bloomed all throughout the year. Being a tropical climate and thus never cold, all you had to do was keep them watered. One day she told Earnest (our first "yard man") to remove the weeds from the flower beds — carefully showing him how to do it. In regards to language let me interject that people in our area didn't know the specific names for individual flowers or trees — just the generic name. If you asked someone what type tree that was, they would say "mti" — this is the Swahili word for tree. In Lou Ann's situation, what did she actually say in Swahili? Or what did Earnest hear her say? Well, by now I'm sure you're well ahead of me. You're right. When Lou Ann returned from the hospital, Earnest had removed the weeds ……. and the flowers — all quite meticulously. Will there be a next time for such a snafu? Of course there will.

"MY GUARDIAN ANGEL"

"Ability is what you're capable of doing; motivation determines what you do; attitude determines how well you do it."

– L. Holtz

I 've told you that I studied harder in Swahili language school than at any time since medical school. Not being a good language learner, I was determined to beat it to death through study. Learning through my "BF" technique (that's "brute force"), I can attest that it was only marginally successful. I can also attest that I was driving Lou Ann loony tunes with my incessant studying. I needed some type of break. In the USA I was always quite active physically despite what might be going on — even in Medical School. This was my diversion and helped keep me sane. But while in school in Morogoro there were few physical activities available. Besides, I was studying during virtually all waking moments. Then the opportunity came to climb the mountains behind our school compound. They rose close to 5000 feet above the valley. Five of the guys were tackling the mountains one Saturday. Lou Ann encouraged me to join the group — I think just to get me out of her hair for a day. But realistically she knew that my mood would improve with a diversion and some good exercise.

The six of us launched out just before daylight the next Saturday. We each took a gallon of water and some snack foods. It was early November and at the end of the dry season. And I do mean dry! The area hadn't seen any rain in about five months. We didn't expect to find any water — much less drinkable water. There was a paucity of green but a super abundance of brown tangled undergrowth. We had to make our own trail through this maze. I should tell you that not only was it the dry season, but it was approaching the hottest time of the year (around 100 degrees Fahrenheit).

We made good progress early in the day when it was relatively cooler, and we just took the path of least resistance as we continued up. If the going became too steep or difficult with undergrowth, we just traversed around it. Not too bad. We trudged on as we aimed at what we thought was the pinnacle of the tallest mountain. Going was slow with the circuitous route and the ever increasing heat. It was past mid-day as we topped out on the 'pinnacle'. As those of you experienced in mountain climbing can attest, our supposed pinnacle turned out to be only a high ridge. Several other higher ridges lay beyond before reaching the actual summit. Decision time. Besides, I finished my gallon of water as we stopped at this point. Uh-oh! Our impending decision was really quite easy. Despite our desire to summit, fortunately good sense prevailed. We had to start back in order to get down before darkness overtook us and the ravages of dehydration began.

Our leader was the most daring man among us and the one in the best physical shape. *"Charge onward"*, he said. Let me remind you that there were no trails, plus it was basically impossible to retrace the route of our ascent. How hard can it be? Just go down, right! Not really. We came upon a number of cliffs that had to be circumvented. *"Where were these when we were climbing?"* I can still see our fearless leader climbing some trees so as to see a better route down. A couple times rather than circle all the way around a near vertical cliff, we jumped from the precipice onto a tree growing from below. Then we'd climb down the tree. Well, that's one way of defeating a cliff. At one point we were walking single file on a narrow ledge overlooking a thirty foot cliff. The undergrowth was so heavy that we couldn't see the person ahead of us. I knew that our fearless leader was ahead of me and had taken a sharp right-handed turn on the narrow ledge, bypassing a rocky promontory. I grasped a dangling vine as I planted my left foot on the ledge — readying myself to turn around the boulder. Then it instantaneously happened. I was falling down the cliff. I didn't know what had happened but now only saw the irregular boulders far below. I was still grasping the vine that had apparently broken. All the while (2-3 seconds) I was deciding how I wanted to hit. At least I was going down feet first, so I thought perhaps I might escape with only a broken ankle. It seemed as if I waited and waited to hit. Then I stopped in midair! What in the world? The vine I had been grasping had apparently caught on something just before my impact. I dangled suspended only about two feet from the rocks. I merely let go the vine and easily dropped down. Amazed and fantastically relieved, I just walked off in the direction of our leader who had obviously come down another way. He saw me and said, *"Where'd you come from."* *"You won't believe this, I said; but....."* I told him and the others what had happened. Because of the dense growth, no one had seen me fall.

In reconstructing the mishap, apparently the rock that I had placed my left foot on just gave way at that moment. Since all my weight was on that leg, down the cliff I went. The vine that was meant to be my stabilizing force apparently also gave way. Now don't ask me why, but I continued to firmly grasp the vine. It turned out to be my <u>savior</u> as it again caught in the tree. Lou Ann says, *"Your guardian angel held you up."* All I had to show for the fall were skinned hands, resulting from the abrasive force on the vine as I jerked to a stop. Thank you God. I could have been injured severely, and my missionary medicine desires could have been dashed before they started.

To finish my mountain climbing story. Remember that most of us had no water for the descent. I was becoming not only quite thirsty but very tired and weak. By chance we came upon a small pool of water at the base of a shaded cliff. Decision time again — to drink the much needed water and risk sickness or to risk further dehydration and possible injury. One of the men produced some iodine tablets. These rendered it "no decision" for me. In other words, "I'll drink the iodinized water". If any of you have ever tasted iodine, it tastes medicinal and is most unpleasant. But in this situation, it was a must. I can't say it tasted good, but I definitely felt better after the water. (None of us got sick later).

It was now getting dark, but it didn't matter. We were nearly down and could see the lights from the school. As we reached the road at the bottom and trudged the last quarter mile to our dorms, my feet and legs felt wooden and unsteady. But we all made it! No harm — no foul. I don't think Lou Ann will be asking me to take any more such outings. And she won't be convinced that my guardian angel didn't hold that vine for me — nor should she!

CULTURE "SHOCK"

"Life is not so much the pursuit of happiness, but the happiness of pursuit. Happiness is essentially and inevitably a by-product."

Okay, everyone knows the term "culture shock" and thinks they understand the concept. Maybe; but the nuances continue to defy even those who regularly deal with changing cultures. Right off the bat; why did I put "shock" in parentheses in the chapter title? Even though it's a catchy term, I think it's a misnomer. I'll tell you why. First of all; what does the word "shock" itself imply to you? Right. It implies something sudden and perhaps drastic or unexpected. Medically when a patient is in shock, it's a dire situation. Something must be done immediately to try and correct it. It is a short-term condition. It is either corrected or not. Patients don't remain in this state. This helps explain why the term "culture shock" is a misnomer. It's not a sudden event that has an ending — it's ongoing in various ways and degrees.

Let me give another analogy. You frequently hear about the stress of parents during their kids' teenage years. It's an ongoing stressful time. You don't hear parents talk about "teenage shock", but rather the stress of the teenage years or "teenage stress". So it is with living in another culture. It's a matter of stress — "culture stress".

By the way, I don't take credit for the term "culture stress". Having read about living in different cultures in various references, I came across this term in one of them. I immediately thought, RIGHT; this is the way it should be defined. While I'm giving disclaimers, I certainly don't intend for this to be any complete and thorough delving into the topic.

Implicit in the term "shock" then is that it is temporary — and self limited. This is exactly why the use of the word "shock" is not accurate for living in a different culture. Of course any new and different culture will have an immediate effect, and this probably explains the origin of the term. But living in a different culture means so much more — much more that is ongoing, changing, but always there to some degree.

I think this immediate effect (the "shock" value) is dulled or softened somewhat by the preparation most people have before living in a different culture. This phrase I coined fits here:

"Just as a picture is worth a thousand words, so is a visit worth a thousand pictures."

My corollary to this is: *"Living in another culture is worth multiple short-term visits"*.

So I use the term "culture stress". We all know what stress is and experience it in most areas of our lives. You can magnify this many times over when living in a different and foreign culture. Some stress is always there in one form or another and at one time or another. It just is, and you cannot escape it. As soon as you realize this, the better off you are and the better you live with the stress. We never get over all forms of culture stress. It can rise up to bite you at the most unexpected times.

Some of the more common ways that culture stress is experienced and felt:

Feeling 'out of sorts'; ill at ease; don't know what you're supposed to do; concerned about offending; did I say that right?; is this the way they say it here?; a feeling of being powerless/no control; did I do the right thing?; I'm so tired of trying to 'hear' the language; why are they doing that?; if someone breaks in line just one more time, I'll….; prejudice, racism, bigotry; cultural cues and clues; bribery; why can't I get this fixed?; when your sense of humor runs out; what to do if _____?; I don't know how to handle this; and so many other situations.

One person may have difficulty with one area of the culture and someone else in another. You think you have it under control and "wham" — no you don't. Some stressors seem to have been overcome but then recur and hit you again. Oh sure it gets less and less as you live there longer, but look out! It will return in some area at some time — often totally unexpected.

Either you compensate and improve your cultural adaptation over time or else you begin to dislike the people and your situation more and more. You begin not to care, and you lose sight of why you came. You become less effective. With some legitimate sounding excuse some people choose to leave. Worse yet; some people become cynical and speak badly about the people and their culture. Someone in this latter condition should leave, for they are damaging both themselves and the local people. Also they are a bad influence on other ex-patriots and may deter other workers from coming.

Some personal areas of culture stress:

- Language — Language: ??!@?&#!??
  I just hate those who "pick it up" so quickly, don't you. No seriously; it's a gift they're born with — like someone who can "play by ear" on a musical instrument. I'm happy for them, and it's a gift I'd dearly love to have. Sometimes your brain just can't take in any more of the language. It becomes very tiring trying to "hear" or translate your new language. I've always said I was in the line getting left handed and red hair when the gift of language learning was handed out. I constantly struggled mightily in Swahili. This was always a source of stress for me. (see chapter on "Language School")

- Efficiency: I pride myself on being efficient. Not so in our new culture, so it was a constant struggle for me. (See chapter on "Efficiency")

- "Losing it": Don't worry; at some point we all lose it. We just can't take it anymore. An example would be at the Post Office when the clerk keeps taking everyone ahead of me — including those who have broken in line. Why is it that we always find ourselves at the back of the line at Customs when we arrive in Dar es Salaam? Keep cool. Don't be the Ugly American.
- Patience: No one seems more patient than the Tanzanians. They wait in line for everything. This is one area that can be a real challenge. But it's an area where I improved a lot. I always took something with me to do or to read while I waited. Upon going back to America I found myself more patient in some areas; but alas, less patient in others. Lou Ann can tell you. Don't ask her.

- Time: This is an area where I failed. In Tanzania time is relative; whereas in the USA we're very time conscious and quite punctual. I must admit I never got used to things starting an hour later that stated. We called it *"African time"*. I had no control over this. The only thing I could do was begin on time when I was in charge. I could not do what some recommend for missionaries: leave your watch at home.

- "Appropriate Assertiveness": In another culture you can't just be a "door mat". You shouldn't be totally passive so as not to appear pushy or too aggressive. It's a good way to not get anything done. I came up with the term "appropriate assertiveness" or you might call it "pleasant assertiveness". Don't show anger, hostility, or haughtiness; and certainly don't shout. Once again; don't be the Ugly American. This behavior will get you nowhere — except to be at the back of the line with nothing accomplished. Just be patient and persistent. Persistent. Much easier said than done.

- "Personal Space": Every culture has its unspoken rules of personal space. In the USA we generally speak and sit at a certain distance from each other. In Tanzania it's much closer — especially sitting in groups such as in a vehicle or in church. There's always room for one more. When driving our vehicle and someone wanted a ride, we could never say *"We're full"*. To the Tanzanian you are never full. I admit this was difficult for me, and I did only fairly well.

MURPHY'S LAWS OF INTERNATIONAL TRAVEL

"The really happy person is the one who can enjoy the scenery when he has to take a detour."

M any of you have had more experience in international travel than we have. You could concoct your own (perhaps better) list. In fact, feel free to add to my list. Ol' Murphy most certainly traveled a lot. His Law, *"If things can go wrong, they will"*, is never more true than in long range travel through various airports and countries. You have to expect this and "roll with the punches". Be flexible. Certainly more easily said than done when the fatigue of travel sets in: lack of sleep, poor airplane food, the inability of getting supine (lying down), toting bags about, a numb derriere, swollen feet, dirty and rumpled clothes, and on and on. A pleasant demeanor seems remote as irritation and impatience loom to the forefront. At this point I always try to remember my favorite quote once again: *"If it's funny later; it's funny now."* Right! Statistically speaking, Murphy's Law wins out about 80% of the time. Occasionally, just occasionally you'll beat him. Come on; check me out on this.

- Jet lag: Jet lag is real. Murphy has nothing to do with this. It's basically just plain old fatigue — the fatigue caused by loss of sleep and complicated by what I call stagnation (not being able to move around freely). Another factor not mentioned as you read about jet lag is the effect of the constant motion and noise of jet travel. Add some of the other factors I mentioned and what do you get à jet lag. There are good references on what to do to minimize this malady. I recommend many of those. When I depart for a different time zone, I set my watch for the time at my destination and begin to think in that regard. Sleep on the plane — if you can. I can't. When you arrive, it's best to "gut it out" that first day — stay up and be active. If you do have a chance for a nap, keep it short (2-3 hours maximum); then go to bed early that first night.

- Life's necessities: Water. After begging for water from an airline attendant who seems affronted or too busy, you get this measly small glass — two swallows at the most. Moral to this story: take your own container of water. However, Murphy may demand you dump it out before boarding. Yes, this has happened to me on numerous occasions.

- Law of Lines: Whatever line you choose; it turns out to be the slowest. When waiting in the passport check line in Africa (you pick the airport), you virtually always find yourself at the end of the line. The locals become very adept at silently slithering in line in front of you. In not wanting to be the "Ugly American", keep smiling and praying for more patience. Well maybe you're beyond smiling at this point.

- Gates: Whatever gate your plane arrives in turns out to be the furthest away from where you go next. At times you may think you've beaten Murphy only to find out the opposite. For example, your new gate may be number 5; and you think, "Wow, we don't *have far to go*." Then you find out this particular airport's numbering system starts their Gate number 1 at the farrrrr end, and there are 34 gates in that wing. Or perhaps you arrive at Gate 7 and depart from Gate 12 (same airline carrier). You're excited. Wow, not far to go! No. As you walk along your concourse, it stops at Gate 10, makes a right hand turn, and for the next half mile you pass numerous shops before gate 12 appears. Whew. Just made it; they're boarding.

  Beware late gate changes. Watch the board; ask. You know how you can depend on those scratchy, garbled announcements in their 'broken English.' — ha. You can find yourself stranded in Lagos, Nigeria, as nearly happened to us once.

- Don't you love that most unwanted announcement, *"There is a slight delay."* Murphy's here.

- Luggage: The last luggage to arrive is yours. Or more typically — one bag didn't arrive, and it's yours. The bag that gets chewed up in the conveyor system is yours.

- Planing and de-planing: First on; last off. Last on; last off.

- Seating: Who gets to sit by the crying child? Who has the seat next to the 350 pound guy? Lou Ann and I have the uncanny ability of being assigned the very back seats — no matter what seats I think I've designated. Those seats often don't recline; they're 'bouncier'; and then there's the proximity of the restroom — complete with the olfactory aroma and the seemingly constant 'whooosh' sound.

- Food: To eat the meals on an airplane you need the skill of a brain surgeon and the athletic dexterity of Michael Jordan. And then there's the — *"Oh sir, we just ran out of the chicken; we only have ——— left."* You fill in the blank. Remember, Murphy is in charge; so what's left is your least favorite dish — one that makes you sick or breaks you out in hives.

- Audio and Video: The system that doesn't work is yours. *"Sorry sir; there's nothing we can do."* — My solution; take your own computer with music and videos. Also, take a good book (or your electronic reader).

- Sleep: First of all; good luck. Perhaps you've finally gotten comfortable and are sleeping when the person behind you slams your seat or the one beside you has a bathroom urge. You're the lucky one near the 2 year old. You know what happens at some point. Finally sleep comes; and the attendant says, *"Put your seat in the upright position for landing."* Then you circle for an hour awaiting the landing. I'm sure being in the "upright" position will protect you so much more if you were to slam into the ground going 350+ miles per hour. But pardon my cynicism.

- Flight delays — missed connections: ?!?@#??# I won't even go there.

General rules (and truisms):

- Hurry up and wait

- Take all you need; use all you take

- You take it; you carry it (without moaning, whining, or complaining)

- Put new batteries in your items (plus extra batteries)

- Everything that is essential and you 'must have' stays in your carry-on.

- Essential items:
    - Patience: Above all, patience

    - Pleasantness: Everyone else is just as tired and uncomfortable as you are.

    - "Appropriate Assertiveness": I coined this term to describe the manner we should assume with agents at airports or in offices. (I wrote about this in the chapter on "Culture Shock.") What to do? Just stand your ground at a proper distance — don't retreat. Maintain some occasional eye contact. Intersperse occasional comments such as, *"How is it going now? Am I* next? *Will it be much longer?"* Remember; they are in charge.

OUR HOUSE

A lot of people ask about our house and our living conditions. Actually the house was constructed for us, and a sign at the front door said, "Black's House". Elsewhere I tell about how this was misinterpreted — you can figure it out. To avoid confusion we took the wooden placard down. The house was quite adequate for us — measuring about 20x40 feet. It was on a concrete slab and constructed with brick fired in a kiln on the compound. The brick is made from dirt obtained from the huge termite mounds. The front door led to the living room area which joined the dining area. The kitchen was next to the dining room. We had two bedrooms and one bathroom with a shower. We used the larger bedroom ourselves and the smaller one as an office — or as a bedroom when we had guests. Both bedrooms had closets in them. As you can see, this was more than adequate. We did add covered front and back porches the first year. Also a storeroom and a wash room in the back.

The water from our faucets was straight from the river. There was a canal dug from the river to a holding tank, which then by gravity fed down to our house. During rainy season we took our showers in the brown water. Because we couldn't drink the river water, we boiled and filtered. Our trusty Katadyn water filter removed all noxious particles, including bacteria. We boiled in order to remove the viruses — such as hepatitis. People lived high on the mountain behind us and used the same river water — a source of contamination. Hot water? No, we didn't have any initially. There was a system set up for hot water, but we chose not to use it. It consisted of a 55 gallon drum mounted on a brick base. The procedure was to build a wood fire below the drum and heat the water. It was then gravity fed by piping from the barrel into our pipes. We chose not to do this because we didn't want to contribute to de-forestation by burning wood every day. Later when National power came to Chimala, we used an electrically powered coil apparatus that wrapped around the pipe above the shower head. This way we could at least get somewhat of a warm trickle of a shower.

Actually our best water was during rainy season (about six months of rain and six months without rain). Of course our pipes ran brown with river water during rainy season. How would you like to take a shower in brown water? As to our best water, we collected rain water in 55 gallon drums from our roof (cistern style). This was our cleanest, best tasting water.

Our first two years we had electrical power only from the compound generator. This generator powered the needs on the mission and ran from 6-9AM and 6-11PM. It was barely enough power to preserve the perishables in our refrigerator and freezer. It did help us in the mornings and the evenings with our various needs. After 11PM if we needed electricity at the hospital, we had to get the guard who was authorized to start the generator. There was often a 30 minute delay. Until the generator started we relied on lanterns and flashlights at the hospital. Some time later we purchased a small Honda generator for use at the hospital. We had it wired for use in the lab, Minor Theatre, and Major Theatre (operating room).

When thinking of our house, I always think of the pleasure we derived from our tin roof — the lovely sound of rain. I must admit that the first time we had hail, however; I was rather startled. In Swahili it's called "mawe", which means "stones". You can imagine the noise.

A/C; what's that? There was no thought of an air conditioner to cool our house. It took expensive diesel to run our compound generator, and the 'draw' of electricity was too great. Besides, remember that initially the generator didn't run at night when we were sleeping. When National Power first came, it was too expensive and of course iffy.

Let me liven up this chapter and tell you of some strange happenings in our house. These occurrences involved creatures which definitely didn't fall into the category of 'friends', like the geckos. As our house was not mosquito-proof, also it was not bat-proof. Somehow, whether by osmosis or spontaneous generation, we would suddenly be aware of a bat flying through the house. It wanted out as much as we wanted it out. They were most skillful in navigating from room to room. What to do? I guess most folks would simply have opened a door, and the bats would make their happy departure. I found another (more gross) way. Shall I say that I played tennis on our compound and found the answer with my tennis racquet. I have a deft backhand, if I do say so myself. By timing their flight path just right while quietly poised in readiness, I could skillfully dispose of the critters with one powerful backhand. I always carefully removed them, for they are known carriers of rabies.

One bat proved to be a mystery. As it was curiously checking out our house, it flew into our bedroom and didn't return. I searched high and low and couldn't find the infernal thing. Being bed time we just gave up and hit the rack under our ever protective mosquito net. The night passed with a pleasant calmness, but such times can be deceiving. I began getting ready for the day. Always being the cautious one, I knock out my shoes habitually — to avoid any surprise by crawling critters. I had my pants draped over a chair and performed the same ritual — shaking them out. To my fright and amazement the lost bat flew out of one of the pant legs. Whew! Was I immediately gratified about my habit! Just think of the possibilities. On second thought; don't. I quickly disposed of the bat and carried on. ——- Africa is always full of surprises and is definitely not for the squeamish or faint of heart.

Ok, another bat story. First let me interject that we used our mosquito net religiously. This would be in spite of Lou Ann saying, "Frank, I can't stand it; it's too hot." Since we couldn't rid our house of mosquitoes, a net was absolutely necessary in this malaria infested location. It also served its purpose against other unwanted pests. I'll bet you're ahead of me now. We were awakened one night to the sound of flopping and movement emanating from the net. I brought out my ever present AA Maglite. You're right; a bat with faulty radar was caught. I dispatched it in the usual way. Oh well, another unexpected but normal occurrence. Back to sleep.

One last bat story. One day at dusk I was outside our house and happened to look up toward the roof. A small ventilation window is located near the roof apex. Before I tell you more I'll tell you what Lou Ann saw. She happened to be looking out the window as this very moment. She said I was just walking along when all of a sudden she saw me fall to the ground. She didn't have any idea what was going on. Had I had an apoplectic attack or been felled by some unknown object? None of the above. She hadn't seen what I saw from my vantage point. As I was looking toward the small window, suddenly a hoard of bats came diving out the window and were seemingly aiming directly at my head. Apparently at some signal the mass of flying mammals departed our attic for their nightly feeding frenzy. I just happened to be in their flight trajectory. They missed me.

Actually we like the bats. They eat innumerable malaria carrying mosquitoes. We just don't like them in our house. After the above episode, I had our workers repair the entrances to our attic one evening — after their mass departure. This also cured the bats from winding up in our house and thus the need for my formidable backhand. We never did figure out how they got through the ceiling board. All holes and tiny cracks had been covered. Another African mystery goes unsolved.

Shall I tell you the 'strange rat' story? Sure. One evening we were sitting in our living room just talking with some friends. Someone noticed a rat slowly sauntering along by the bookshelves and headed to the kitchen. Of course this is very strange behavior. I thought the rat must be sick or had gotten poison. I quickly went to get our broom to flummox the rascal. By the time I got back we couldn't find it in the kitchen. As with the bat, we had to give up looking. Several days passed. One afternoon Zebron, our cook, said there was a foul smell in the kitchen. He and Lou Ann proceeded to look and look — nothing. Then Zebron took off one of the burners of our gas stove. There curled up around the gas jet, partially burned, and quite dead lay the rat. Yuck is right. Can you even imagine such a thing in your house?

So you like to walk barefoot in your house like my wife. Well, she gave it up, and I'll tell you why. We had these huge — I mean huge — very fast spiders which invaded us. We called them "wind scorpions"; perhaps denoting their speed. They're also called camel spiders and carry a vicious bite. I think they broke the sound barrier with their speed — very intimidating. Consequently, they were very difficult to curtail. To smash them on the floor not only took dexterity, but the result was a juicy mess (sorry to be gross). I feel sure you'd give up walking barefoot also.

Despite it all, we found our house more than adequate and really enjoyed living there. It became not just our house but our home. There are so many adventures and unusual things just living at Chimala — separate and apart from the strange and tragic events at the hospital. So many memories.

OUR VEHICLE & ROADWAY HAZARDS

*"Just as a picture is worth a thousand words;
so is a visit worth a thousand pictures."*

– Frank Black

When we first arrived in Tanzania in July 1992, our new Toyota Land Cruiser was in port waiting for us. I had ordered the vehicle from Japan several months before and had it shipped to Dar es Salaam. The entire process had worked as smooth as silk. However, there was one slight problem. For whatever reason, the Department that controlled the duty on incoming vehicles had decided that missionaries were to pay the same duty as businesses or individuals before the vehicles would be released. Before this there had been no duty on incoming missionary vehicles. And I'm talking no small amount of money here. The duty that was now being asked could run as high as 20-30% of the vehicle's cost. You can see this was prohibitive. Consequently, many vehicles including ours had been impounded in the port. In the meantime the Lutheran, Catholic, and Baptist leaders were working with the government in order to rescind this new directive. But what were we to do, and how were we going to get around?

I will forever be grateful to John and Jan Boren. They were yearly visitors to Chimala Mission and had bought a Land Cruiser that had been off-loaded prior to the duty change. John and Jan were not in Tanzania at this time; so they told me I could get their brand new, fancy Land Cruiser from the port and use it. Seriously now, would you do this? It was amazingly generous of them! Remember that I had NEVER driven "British style" (a right hand drive vehicle on the left side of the road). Of course I'd been driving for decades but just imagine driving someone else's new vehicle in this situation. I was just as nervous as when I was a beginning sixteen year old driver.

You can also add in these significant factors: roadway conditions, the crowds, animals on the roadway, poor drivers who don't honor what few road rules that exist, poor vehicles, etc. My very first outing was to drive some three hours to Morogoro, where we went to language school. Anxiety personified! I did make one 'amateur' mistake on that journey. I made the mistake of parking with one side of the car near a wall. I found out later that you never do this, for people can come between the wall and the car to break in unseen. You're supposed to park so that both sides can be equally seen. You guessed it. Someone tried to break in the driver's side door. I think they got interrupted somehow, for they didn't get in the vehicle. They did succeed in breaking the lock. I was embarrassed but quite glad nothing worse had happened — like having the vehicle stolen! Fortunately I was able to rather quickly get a new lock on the door.

About a month later the new duty was rescinded, and I was able to get our vehicle. By then I was comfortable driving in this "new style", but an added comfort was having our own vehicle. Lou Ann and I were used to driving a stick shift, but of course our new vehicle had the shift on the left side. Most everything at first felt backwards — the gear shift on the left, the blinker lever on the right, rear view mirror on the left, driving on the left side, wiper controls on the left, etc. You'd never guess what was the hardest to get used to — it was looking up to the left into the rear view mirror. When in a hurry, I couldn't tell you how many times the wipers would start going when actually we had wanted to start blinking.

Flats — punctures. These became the bane of travel. In the USA you might drive for years and never have a flat. They became routine for us. We virtually never made any lengthy trip without a good puncture or two. You might wonder why we had so many flats. The roads were littered with bits of wood, metal, glass, nails, screws, bolts, huge thorns, etc. But we were prepared. We had tire plug kits, tube puncture kits, extra tubes and tires (we sometimes put tubes in 'tubeless tires'), and an air pump that worked off the electrical system. The system of changing tires is a bit cumbersome on the Land Cruiser, but I mastered it and changed tires in record time. Vehicles were often stolen when you were stopped to change flats. This is why I became so proficient. Lou Ann served as my lookout, and I was fully prepared to drive away in a partially disabled vehicle with a puncture.

We ordered our vehicle with the "off road package." It had an extra strong suspension, special under carriage, and an auxiliary diesel tank (we had a range of some 500 miles). I never did test this distance however — usually seeking to refuel by the time the tank was down to one-third. Stations with fuel were uncertain and far between. Our over used top carrier was tested to the breaking point on many occasions — our Land Cruiser being a true "beast of burden". Where there were speed signs, the maximum speed was 100 kilometers per hour (63 miles per hour). We rarely exceeded this speed. There were just too many uncertainties: bad to worse roads; obstacles in the road as mentioned (add in wrecked vehicles to stalled vehicles to animals to people, etc.). Many vehicles were in bad repair and with poor drivers, worse tires, speeding, and being over loaded; they were a disaster waiting to happen. All these reasons and more are why the roadway was our greatest hazard. We personally know two missionaries who were killed on the roadway and a third with permanent brain damage. The roadway was our greatest hazard without doubt — not malaria, thieves, revolution, snakes, or other.

There is one thing in a vehicle in Third World I would not do without. Care to guess what that is? It's a good functioning air conditioner. Now lest you think that I just have to have cool comfort, there are other factors. (I grew up in Tennessee without an air conditioned house or car. As a matter of fact, it was 1969 before we had A/C in a car). A/C allows you to be comfortable of course; but with the windows closed you can avoid dust, most of diesel fumes, and other odors. A factor you probably wouldn't think about is safety. What do I mean you ask? When you are stopped around crowds, it's amazing how many hands reach through open windows — trying to sell you things or grab things. Once in Dar es Salaam while stopped in traffic we saw the watch ripped off the arm of a lady ahead of us — her window was down. He dashed off in the crowd. It was also just as important to always keep our doors locked. Frequently in crowds we'd have people try and open our doors.

Our Land Cruiser was a fantastic vehicle. It only had one problem. There was a slight leak in the A/C fluid. It would keep us cool from Chimala to Dar (500 miles), and then it would peter out. Dar is coastal and therefore very hot and humid. On several trips to Dar I would try different places who ostensibly worked on air conditioners. I would have it "fixed" and recharged. But, alas, the problem kept recurring. It wasn't fixed. Finally someone found a slight leak in the system, and it remained fixed. This brings up another point about our USA world and the developing world. This has to do with *Services* of all types. We can pretty much depend on good services in the USA (whether it's cars, plumbing, electrical, garage doors, etc.). Not so in the developing countries. Of course the workers will all say, *"Oh, no problem, I can fix it"*. We found out this is probably cultural and certainly not the case.

We did get two tickets. One was a speeding ticket as I was exiting a town. "Speed guns" seemed to be a new toy, and this is what got me. I was probably going 40mph in a 30mph zone. I knew better than to give the money to the police (it would be pocketed). I asked to go to the Police Station to pay — the money probably just wound up in different pockets. Our other ticket was a simple police check, which were all too frequent. As obvious non-Tanzanians we were definitely targeted. The police would check our licenses, passports, car stickers, lights, etc. This particular officer could find nothing. Then he looked inside our vehicle one more time. By now we'd been stopped for probably ten minutes. Lou Ann had taken off her seat belt to reach in the back and get some food. Of course we always wore our seat belts! He said, *"Oh, she is not wearing belt."* Explanations fell on deaf ears; and yes, we had to pay a fine for not wearing seat belts. Really ludicrous when you think about it in this setting with their unsafe roadways. But once again we were victims of wazungu (white people) discrimination. We learned many times over what it's like to be in the minority and without any recourse.

In our years of driving we had just one mishap. I hit and killed a goat. It was the straggler behind several others crossing the road. I know to always look for a straggler — this time I didn't. When it comes to "road kill" stories, I can always "one up" everyone. What am I talking about? Here's the story:

We were headed from Dar to Chimala one early morning and happened to be on the portion of the main road that traverses Mikumi Game Park. Up ahead we could see a number of vehicles and people in the roadway. This often means the sighting of a number of animals. Not this time. About now I saw what appeared to be blood on the roadway. As I was trying to figure it out, I saw a large grayish mound on the left side of the road. It was an elephant — a dead elephant. I then looked to the right side of the roadway and saw a large over turned truck. It wasn't difficult to put together what had happened. Unfortunately, the truck driver also had died. You might be thinking, *"How in the world can you hit something as big as an elephant?"* It probably had occurred about dawn when visibility is poor. Elephants are surprisingly fast, and it had probably emerged quickly onto the roadway from the tall grasses that line the road. These grasses are called "elephant grass" by the way — they do reach the height of an elephant and are similar in color. Now you can see how this might happen. (I have pictures to prove my story)

CULTURAL DIFFERENCES

"An empty stomach has no ears."
— African Proverb

F irst of all, let me be quite clear as I try and carefully point out that these are merely my observations. I am not being judgmental and certainly am not claiming any superior intelligence or position. This is the furthest thing from my thinking. Sure our cultures are different. But that's it. Different; yes. Better; no. There's no right or wrong; no superior or inferior position. Just different. If I've worded things poorly, please do not assume my motives. My writing reflects my thinking, which was always one of *perspective* — looking at differences in cultures, never with the thought of judgmental comparison.

Racial Prejudice:

If anything, the Tanzanians had "reverse racial prejudice". In other words, they often thought of us whites ahead of their own — as being more intelligent, better trained, more capable of leading, richer, etc. I suppose this grew out of the period when the Portuguese, Germans, and British were the colonial powers. As far as giving us whites the predominant position, part of it would also be due to the graciousness of the Tanzanian people. I always say and want to say again that I found this to be most humbling. The Tanzanians would actually choose to see me (as their physician) over one of their own. I want to quickly point out that Lou Ann and I felt no personal racial discrimination in Tanzania. And the reverse is equally true. We felt no prejudice towards the Tanzanians. It is true that we had the blessing of location (USA) and our families — resulting in more education, travel, and other experiences. Because we had certain advantages, we felt more responsibility — more obligation to help.

When I would show up at a church service, it was inevitable that the leaders would ask me to speak. Again, I think this was more a common courtesy and part of their cultural practice. (If they knew my speaking ability, they might have reconsidered.). I appreciated their requests and never went without my Bible and some notes from which to speak. I refused on only one occasion. I was in a large city in a church that had about 700 people present. I was the only white in the building. Talk about feeling in the minority! I had a seat toward the back of the auditorium and prepared myself to listen to their well known minister. I thought for sure that this would be the one time I would not be asked to speak. This large church had several full-time ministers and a very impressive group of professional men as leaders. But just before the worship services were to begin I saw several of the leaders conferring. Then one of them began walking my way. Uh-oh, I knew then that he was going to ask me to speak. I was right but had my answer ready. I said, *"Thank you very much, but I'm just visiting. I've been looking forward to listening to your minister, so I graciously decline."*

Personal Habits:

Spitting, burping, passing gas, coughing without covering your mouth, nose picking, staring. These are all accepted public behaviors for both men and women. I always found it difficult to keep a straight face when I was in the office of a Government official, and they began digging at their nose. It was rather difficult to concentrate.

Regarding coughing: all the hospital staff can still hear me yelling in the wards, *"Funga mdomo unapokohoa."* This means, *"Cover your mouth when you cough."* Remember, we had an open ward with all types of patients mixed together. Every American child knows to cover his mouth, for coughing spreads disease. This was not part of the Tanzanian mindset.

Tanzanians eat with their hands and don't use utensils. Very practical don't you think? It's cheaper and those utensils (hands) are always with you. I must admit that I had some trouble with this — and you might as well. Their diet every single day consisted chiefly of ugali — which is like a stiff mush made of corn. They would make a ball with their hands and pop it in their mouth. If they had some soup with their meal, they made a depression in the ball of mush with their thumb and filled it with the liquid. Got the picture?

Sharing Information or Skills:

It seemed the norm for Tanzanians to have a hesitance in sharing their knowledge and abilities with their co-workers — even new workers. In our American culture our bent is to help a newcomer or anyone with less experience — to be a teacher. I didn't know what to make of this. It's almost like they were saying, *"I worked hard to learn this, and I'm not going to make it easier for you."* Also I wondered if they wanted to feel superior in some way. I can only speculate about the reasons. It's just that it was quite noticeable and so different from our culture. We feel it is our responsibility to teach or help others.

Somewhat the opposite of the above is the difficulty Tanzanians seemed to have in disciplining one of their own. This was true even when part of someone's responsibility was to supervise. Again, I can only speculate regarding the reasons. Let me give you an example. We had a Medical Assistant who was a very poor clinician, suspected to be dishonest, and abused alcohol. I feel certain his hospital co-workers were fully aware of these traits and more. One evening he could not be reached by the midwives. He was on first call, and I was his back-up. So the midwives called me. As I was examining the patient, John (not his name) showed up and smelled strongly of alcohol. I reported him to the Hospital Administrator and subsequently to the Labor Relations Committee (comprised of various Hospital Staff). At a subsequent Committee meeting I presented my case, and of course John denied all charges. He was fully exonerated by the Committee with no reprisal.

Their reason? They asked if I had a blood alcohol test. I did not. Case over. We had absolutely zero access to any testing for alcohol.

"Hamna":

Hamna means *"You don't have any."* This seemed to be the stock answer when they didn't know if any items were left — even if they hadn't looked. It drove Lou Ann crazy. But in her sweet manner, she would control other urges and say, *"Have you looked for it?"* or *"Why didn't you tell me you were out?"*

Nurse behavior:

We always had to caution guests regarding how our nurses acted toward their patients. To an American they would appear abrupt, rude, lacking in compassion, and at times downright mean — even punitive. Granted it's hard to understand their actions, but these are entirely cultural differences. Their manner is quite opposite what I see in American nurses (what I call being a "miss nicey nurse").

"Can you fix this?"

The expected, typical Tanzanian answer is *"Yes"*. You virtually never get a *"No"*. It doesn't matter what it is or whether they've ever done it before. Whether experienced or not doesn't seem to enter the equation. We quickly came to realize this cultural trait and that the affirmative "yes" answer could usually be discounted.

A blatant example occurred while in the bottom of the Ngorongoro Crater. I was driving my Toyota Land Cruiser and had the misfortune of hitting one of those gigantic eight inch thorns in a bush along side the road. Immediately the tire deflated. Oops, now what? Remember, this is probably one of the best places in the world to see wild game. And we had just left an area with some lions. Now if you don't know, to change a tire on that model Land Cruiser was no easy task. You had to know how to do it; and even then, it was quite awkward. I asked my guide if he knew how to change the tire. *"Hakuna shida"* (no problem), my guide quickly said, as he jumped out of the vehicle. I told Lou Ann to watch for animals and followed him to the rear of our vehicle. It quickly became apparent that he had absolutely no idea what to do. I reaffirmed to Lou Ann to warn me of any approaching animals as I went about changing the tire. No untoward events occurred, and we continued our tour of the Crater.

Odor:

We Americans have very sensitive noses for noxious odors — especially body odor. This is another reason we're considered "weak" by the Tanzanian — because we don't have a strong body odor. Instead, we have the odor of soap and perfume and hair spray. One author says that a requirement for missionaries is a *"Good sense of humor and a poor sense of smell."*

We recognized that different tribes had different odors about them. No, I'm not being derogatory; we too have our odor. For example, we could always tell the Masaai people. Their effluvium was a rather noxious mixture of body odor, urine, and smoke. The body odor of course is from the heat, sweating, and the lack of bathing and washing their clothes. How would you do in that climate with few clothes and scant water? The urine odor is from their houses, which are made of mud and cow urine — yes, that's true. The smoky odor comes from the open fires in their houses.

Seriously, you do have to adjust your nasal sensitivity and just get used to it — that's the way it is; you're not going to change it. Don't let this gross you out, but I am very good at quickly reverting to mouth breathing. This essentially takes away the odor for me. It really does. Try it. And no, I never think about breathing in particulate matter. In fact, I never thought about it until someone mentioned it.

Spatial relationships:

I'll bet you're thinking this is an unusual thing to mention. I'll explain. I noticed this at various times when we moved furniture from place to place. It seems intuitive to us Americans on how to twist and turn and maneuver furniture to get it through doors or narrow places. We can just envision how it's to be done. It's not this way to Tanzanians. It was comical at times how several men would try and get a chair through a door in some contorted way that obviously would not work. As to why this 'spatial relationship deficit' was present, I have a theory. American children play with puzzles and shapes from their very early years. They develop an understanding of what fits and what doesn't. Tanzanian children simply don't play with such things. Therefore, I think this type knowledge becomes imprinted on our youthful brains and conversely does not with the Tanzanians. What do you think of my theory?

Personal Space:

We Americans like our space — the amount of space between ourselves and others. It's usually in the range of two feet. Just think how uncomfortable you are on an airplane and seated next to a stranger. This is perhaps the closest you come to people you don't know. This type of spacing means nothing to Tanzanians. Cars or benches are never full — there's always room for another — and another. You've seen pictures of trucks or buses laden with sooo many people in developing countries. It's just the way it is. I don't know why; I do know it means nothing to them. You just can't believe how many people can 'scrunch up' together. In church you'd be certain that the bench was full. But no! With a little twisting and turning low and behold another person or two could slide in. They do it so naturally. The Tanzanians assume that our American spacing habits are like theirs. We learned never to say, *"Our car is full and we can't take you."* We'd just have to say, *"Not this time"* — or some such thing.

Staring:

Get used to it. Get used to being stared at — I mean not by one person but many. And it goes on and on. Yes, we got used to it; but this is one thing that newcomers or guests notice right off the bat. Our every action seemed to be of extreme interest. Well after all, what else is there to do? — no TV, no radio, no magazines, no computer screens or games. And after all, us white folks have "things" — all these things we carry with us. There was tremendous interest in the medical bag I always carried (my green Land's End bag). You never knew what I might pull out next. I must admit that I probably did have fifty different items in my all purpose bag — medical and other. That interest may have been superseded only by interest in what I wrote down in my book or the chart. The staff would crane their necks and look over my shoulder to get a better and an immediate look. I always thought, "Can't you wait just a minute." For some reason this continued to bother me.

Language and Women:

I fully confess that I did not have an "ear" for Swahili. (I know; I write about my language deficiency frequently). What I mean is that unless the people spoke quite clearly, succinctly, and loud enough, I had great difficulty catching the meaning. This difficulty was magnified when most women patients spoke to me. They would speak quite softly with their head down — chin on their chest. Obviously this made it even more difficult to understand what they were saying. Consequently, I kept my questions to a minimum, trying to illicit short or even "yes" and "no" answers. As to why the woman did this, I thought it was a combination of respect, shyness, and intimidation. I was an American, male doctor — three strong factors explaining their behavior. They granted me entirely too much homage, and it was most humbling — but it didn't help in understanding them.

Choice and Variety:

Life in the Third World is one of very few choices and less variety. For example, the people of Tanzania ate ugali every day, every day, every day....... Are you bored yet? How would you like to eat the same thing every single day? I don't imagine you'd even like to eat your most favorite food every day. The Tanzanians feel the opposite. A day is not complete unless they have at least one meal with a huge plate of ugali. I've written about their "corn meal mush". Even tiny, thin people would put away a huge, rounded plate of ugali at the evening meal. Amazing! I couldn't eat one-fourth of that amount. It's basically tasteless and to me would be aided greatly by some salt, but they just don't eat it that way. I think part of their enjoying a meal was the tactile part — 'fondling' the ugali into a ball nearly the size of a ping-pong ball. Then with nary a chew the rather large ball of ugali would be swallowed — adding a gustatory pleasure to their meal. There is actually very little food value to their beloved ugali.

The main reason for the lack of variety is simply that things are not available. And even if they were, most people would not have the money to buy them. Think TV stations! How many choices do you have? And now think of someone who does not have a TV nor any hope of getting one. Besides, if they had one, the programming is very elementary and limited.

We like dry cereal with our breakfast at times. The cereal we could buy in Tanzania was quite limited as to type and quality. It was virtually always stale! I said to Lou Ann, "Just don't buy any more cereal." Many times the cereal must have been shipped with soap products. The potency of the perfumes in soap would 'invade' the cereal — making it taste like soap. Both of us would almost gag when a box was opened. And eat it — absolutely not! I can still smell it years later.

OUR "COMPETITION"

"There are no means to which a man will not resort to avoid the real labor of thinking."

— Joshua Reynold

I often refer to the deficiency of the Tanzanian medical system: limited number of care givers; limited medicines and supplies; deficient quality and quantity of training; no restrictions or overview; limited ongoing education; poor peer review. These and other reasons are why we (First World physicians and nurses) are almost revered and certainly preferred by the rank and file Tanzanians over their own doctors. As I always say, *"This is a privilege and most humbling."*

(This is like you preferring an unknown Tanzanian doctor who's first arrived in the USA over your own doctor. Sounds preposterous, doesn't it? But this is an exact analogy. As I've said and it's worth repeating; this is most humbling.)

Our American medicine is generally referred to as "Western Medicine". This is in contrast to what is called "Native Medicine". Native Medicine isn't all about incantations and reading chicken entrails, even though this occurs. The ones who do this would usually be referred to as "witch doctors" by us. They get into the realm of witchcraft, sorcery, sacrifices, etc. Local healers (shamans) generally mean well and are sincere in wanting to help people. They learn their trade by apprenticeship. They generally have many potions made from local plants, trees, various animals and minerals, etc. When I visited such a healer in Chimala, his dark, drab, and musty shop contained a myriad of various jars scattered in some unknown order on irregular shelves. An unknown yet interesting suffusion of odors emanated from the shop. When asked if he had something for snakebite, he would quickly go to a certain section and pick up a jar — assuring us of its curative powers. He did the same when asked about HIV/AIDS, and so on. I would think some of the remedies had a somewhat positive effect, but I strongly suspect that most had little more than an expected 20% placebo effect. Add this effect to God's innate healing built into our bodies, and the "native doctor" would have a dedicated "clientele". I think he believed in the potions and don't think most of such men were shysters. By the way, the monetary charge by these men was often as much as ours — if not more.

These Native Medicine healers were our biggest competition. The local people had been raised by using them and believed in them. Perhaps the people would hear about our medicine and give us a try. Many would freely go back and forth between our Western Medicine and the Native Medicine — staying with whatever seemed to work best. I have no way of knowing how many people came to us preferentially versus how many left us to go to a "native doctor."

Many people came to us with various scratch marks on their bodies. This was a sure sign they had been to a native doctor first. Ostensibly the scratches or small cuts were to relieve an underlying problem — pain, swelling, etc. Perhaps to let the evil "humors" out. We also saw various potions stuck on peoples' heads. These were supposedly for fever or seizures. There was an assortment of amulets or talismans worn on the wrists or as a necklace. These were thought to have some magical power to ward off illness, injury, or evil.

One afternoon at the hospital there was a commotion on female ward. I couldn't ascertain what was going on. Someone ran to Bernard, our administrator, to let him know the situation. He promptly took care of the man at the root of the palaver. It seems that the man was a "witch doctor" and was trying to steal one of our patients. Bernard let me know that he had run him off. — (Competition knows no bounds)

Acute psychosis from a psychiatric etiology is a difficult challenge whether at Chimala or an Indianapolis ER. These patients are confused, disoriented, and often loud and wild. We did have the age old Thorazine injection that would temporarily help. But I'm sorry to say we had little to offer these patients on a long-term basis. The patients' families would usually give us two to three days to "cure" their relative. This was not possible. I'm pretty sure they would then go to their native doctor. The general thinking was that the person had been bewitched and a "spell" cast on them. I well remember one striking case. This man wasn't combative, but he was extremely loud. I can still here his loud *"Shetani toka"* reverberating throughout the hospital from male ward. This translates to, *"Come out Satan"*. His family took him away after the usual couple days when he was no better.

I did a partial intestinal resection on a man who had experienced severe abdominal pain for several days. The segment of intestine removed was necrotic (dead) due to a volvulus (twisting). It's rather foreign to Americans, but Tanzanians like to see the body parts that are removed. I showed the removed portion of intestine to some family members after surgery. The immediate consensus response was that he had been bewitched. Nothing that I said made any difference. Their animistic worldview was simply too ingrained. Unfortunately the man died later that day with severe sepsis.

We made our own IV fluids, and occasionally they would contain some particles that were pyrogenic (fever producing). The fluid was sterilized, but the foreign articles would cause chills and fever in a patient. On one occasion a lady ripped out her IV during such a reaction and refused another one. She said, *"The devil was in the IV fluid."* As was usually the case, she couldn't be convinced otherwise.

I've written a chapter on HIV/AIDS but didn't elucidate the many falsehoods related to the cause. One very prevalent idea was that the sick person had been bewitched. Generally the people just couldn't comprehend the etiology (cause) and course of this unique and horrible disease. Consequently since it was quite obscure, many people turned to their belief in the occult. They would seek out native healers with their various potions and sacrifices. By the way, this was costly to the patient and their families — usually more than our hospital charged. Many families would spend all their money going from "healer to healer" or hospital to hospital. Unfortunately at this time, we also had little to offer patients for the control of HIV/AIDS. We could only try and treat some of the resultant complications and infections.

SURGERY BY A NON-SURGEON

"Success is the ability to go from failure to failure with no loss of enthusiasm."

– Winston Churchill

I performed many surgical procedures at Chimala. Of course in the USA I would not be allowed to do surgery without specialty training. I had my Tanzanian medical license, and there were no restrictions placed on my practice of medicine. That's right. I could do whatever I desired. As I always say, I feel totally humbled by this. The patients would entrust me to help them. What a responsibility! I should add that most of the time there was no other choice for the patient (Infinitely different from the USA). The onus was on me to do what I thought best — surgery included.

I did have some training in surgery in medical school and three months during my Internship. Consequently, I was familiar with anatomy, some surgical techniques, procedures, and instruments — that's not to say that I had performed the cases. Simply stated, basic surgical technique is mechanical and decision making is often practical. Of course I'm over simplifying, for there are infinite variations in situations. My mainstays at Chimala were several surgical texts that described in words how to do cases — some pictures would be added. The old adage in medicine about, *"See one — Do one — Teach one"*, was supplanted at Chimala by *"Read about it and go do it."* Don't laugh now; this is actually what I did on some cases. Seeing the type of surgery that was needed, I would come home and read extensively in my texts and arrive at my surgical approach. The following cases were ones I did having never scrubbed on them before: finger, toe, and leg amputations; hydrocele; testicular torsion; stab wounds to the abdomen; abdominal hernia using mesh; bowel resection; splenectomy; tubal ligation, bladder repair, skin grafting, and ruptured ectopic pregnancy. As I write this it does seem rather amazing, doesn't it? But I want to emphasize again, I was not being careless; and most these cases (with the help of my books) were fairly straight forward using basic surgical techniques. The main books I'm referring to are: 1) <u>Primary Surgery, Volumes One and Two</u> — Edited primarily by Maurice King. (These two volumes were invaluable. They were primarily written for doctors in underdeveloped areas). 2) <u>Complications of Gynecologic and Obstetric Management</u> — by Newton.

Let me tell you one of my favorite surgical stories. This case presented as a ruptured ectopic pregnancy. These are usually a pregnancy in one of the ovarian tubes that ruptures at about ten to twelve weeks. This particular lady presented like most such patients with severe abdominal pain, signs of blood loss, and a positive pregnancy test. I took her to surgery, opened her up, and as suspected found much blood in her abdomen from the ruptured tube — or so I thought. As we were sucking the blood from her abdomen, I saw a small three month sized fetus floating in her abdomen. This was an abdominal pregnancy — meaning that the placenta, umbilical cord, and fetus were all within the abdominal cavity. It was indeed an ectopic pregnancy (meaning outside the uterus), but it was not the usual tubal pregnancy. (I hope you understand that). Upon clearing the blood from her abdomen we could see the placenta attached to her colon and abdominal wall with the umbilical cord and baby attached. The placenta looked rather foreboding, for it is quite vascular. It was attached quite firmly and had a few points of bleeding. In assaying the situation I cut the cord and baby free, then over sewed the bleeding points, and decided to leave the placenta alone. I knew it would either scar down or be somewhat reabsorbed. I closed her in the usual manner, and she did well.

When I went home and looked up abdominal pregnancy in my <u>Williams Textbook of Obstetrics</u> from medical school, I was both flabbergasted and relieved. First of all, abdominal pregnancies are quite rare — occurring about once in 15,000 pregnancies. Then the zinger, and I'll quote from the text: *"The operation for abdominal pregnancy frequently precipitates the most violent and colossal hemorrhage known to surgery."* WHEW!

No, I wasn't lucky; somehow I kind of inherently knew that I should leave the placenta in place. Like I said; some decisions in surgery rely on practical judgment, and thank God for giving me the course to follow in this case.

While I'm at it I'll tell you about another case. This deals with your more usual ectopic pregnancy. This particular lady was in profound shock and unconscious — breathing and with a heart beat but no obtainable blood pressure. We quickly rushed her to the operating theatre, put her on the table, started two IV's with saline wide open, and opened her up. That's right; I quickly gloved, wiped her abdomen with betadine, used some local anesthesia on her skin, and cut her open. We were met with a gush of blood, collecting all we could in our sterile blood bottles. We then began to give her this blood through the IV's (autotransfusion). We got six bottles of blood from her abdomen! This represented about half her total blood volume — the most I ever got from a patient. I tied off the bleeders, sacrificed the one ruptured tube, and closed her. During the procedure she began to be more responsive as her blood pressure increased. At this point we gave her a small amount of general anesthetic. At the end of surgery her pressure had returned to about 90 systolic. She subsequently did well and recovered nicely. The God given strength of the human body is simply amazing! She will live to have another baby.

Anesthesia

The most common anesthetic we used was ketamine. It is an old one that has fallen out of favor in the USA. It is really called a "dissociative anesthetic" and is not truly a general anesthetic. We used it because it's quite safe in most circumstances, it's quick, can be given IV or IM (intravenous or intramuscular), can be used in children and adults, erases any memory of the episode, and requires little training to administer. The downside involves coming out from under the anesthesia. The patient often has very disturbing dreams and thoughts and can become quite wild. We tried to counteract this with IV diazepam (Valium). This is the main reason it fell out of favor in the USA.

We did some surgeries under spinal anesthesia. This would be for cases below the waist. It did take longer to do the procedure (spinal), and then we'd have to wait for the anesthesia to take effect. Also these patients required closer monitoring (blood pressure and level of spinal). Yours truly did have more experience doing them, so I performed the spinals. You can see that in a real emergency situation, this would be very time consuming. I would have to perform the spinal and then go scrub for surgery. This is why we mostly used the quicker and safer ketamine.

SNAKES

"The wise man in the storm prays to God, not for safety from danger, but for deliverance from fear."

One of the most common questions we encountered when home on furlough was, "Do you see snakes?" We would then patiently tell a few snake stories. Yes, we saw snakes — lots of them, especially during the early rainy season. In fact, our house and the area around it seemed to be a breeding ground for cobras. It wasn't at all unusual to see 'baby' cobras on the floor in our house. Yes, in our house! They looked like large earthworms, but their movement gave them away. We always wondered, *"Where'd they come from, and where's their mama?"* I always disposed of them; for as the Africans said, *"The only good snake is a dead snake."* They are dreadfully fearful of snakes and for good reason. About 80% of the snakes in Africa are poisonous; and believe me, they have many snakes. (Whereas, the USA has only four poisonous varieties). We had no antivenom at the hospital, and we could do very little for the unfortunate patients. A bite by a poisonous snake often meant death.

A frightening time occurred with Lou Ann one evening. She and Janice were walking on the roadway in front of Janice's house. Suddenly Lou Ann felt a sharp prick on her left big toe. She knew she'd been bitten by something. A search with their torches (flashlights) revealed a small snake. We were always told to yell, *"Nyoka, nyoka"* (snake, snake), and the night watch would come to kill the snake. He came and did kill it, but in the process its head was crushed. It was a young snake and many types of snakes look similar at this stage. However, often they can be identified by their heads. Because of the condition of the head, we were unable to be certain. We assumed it was a small cobra, for this was by far the most common snake we saw.

(By the way; she had on 'flip-flops' but never wore them again at night.)

We brought Lou Ann back to our house by car and elevated her leg. It was already getting more swollen and painful. We iced the area, gave her benadryl, a steroid, and prayed. The area surrounding the bite rapidly increased in swelling — eventually extending to her knee. She said she could feel the poison going up her body and could even taste it. She felt palpitations and shortness of breath. The worst symptom was the pain in her leg; and the other symptoms gradually abated. It was a very scary time, but all along I thought that she was never in grave danger because of the snake's size (the amount of venom would consequently be small). Of course she was frightened but remained calm. I tried to reassure her that serious reactions (or worse) happened in the first 1-2 hours. This is indeed usually the case with fatalities, even though later she realized that some fatal outcomes occur much later. By the next morning the swelling had stopped at knee level, the pain was still present, and a small black area began to appear at the bite site. Later some skin sloughed off, but the area healed well. The swelling and pain improved and subsided over a few days. We felt blessed; and if possible, became even more watchful for *nyoka*. (We never did have anti-venom during our years at Chimala — hard to obtain and quite expensive)

One of my biggest cultural blunders happened that first morning after the bite. Bernard, our Hospital Administrator, came to our door along with several other men — from the hospital and the church. They had come to see Lou Ann.

(It's true that somehow every happening spreads very rapidly here. We missionaries joked about the Africans knowing when we would be traveling from the compound even before we knew — certainly before we packed our cars, etc. How?)

In being the dutiful husband and trying to let my wife rest (she got very little sleep that first night), I greeted them politely, explained that she was resting, and that she couldn't receive company at this time. WRONG! This was my mistake. It was a cultural "no — no" to do what I did — to not let them in to see her. Bernard said nothing but left with the other men. It was only later that I found out the significance of what I'd done. It took quite some time to overcome my cultural faux pas.

The two biggest snakes I ever saw at Chimala were both within twenty yards of my house! What type? Probably king cobras — as big around as my arm and about eight feet long. One slithered into a hole in front of our house and the other crawled under a large brush pile in the back. I pursued the matter no further — just remaining more on guard, if that were possible.

I never — I said "NEVER" went anywhere at night without my trusty torch (flashlight). As long as you saw the snake first, you could avoid it and yell the proverbial, "*Nyoka — Nyoka*". I also took what I called my "snake stick" with me at night. It's like a four foot long walking stick but much harder. It's made by the Masaai from an African hard wood and repeatedly oiled and heated over a fire. The resulting stick is like an iron rod. Masaai men always carry one as a weapon. By the way, my snake stick killed more than one cobra. My rule of thumb was that if the snake was bigger than my stick, I would summon a guard.

On one occasion as I was returning from night rounds and walking on the sidewalk to our house, I was greeted by a cobra. It was not just crawling along, but it had risen up and flared — most intimidating. Upon yelling the 'magic word' the guard (mlinzi) started the chase. With his trusty machete he was successful in chopping off about a third of the tail end of the rascal. Still it rapidly slithered around in and out of our bushes. Boy are they fast! Occasionally, even missing a significant portion of its length, it was able to rise up and flare. Eventually the guard was successful in his quest, and the snake became a "good snake." I must admit that watching this sequence of events was almost comical.

Another almost comical event happened one day at lunch. We were eating in a small, outside, screened in room. It was the last day for a group of visitors; and one of them commented, *"We've been here an entire month and haven't seen a single snake."* It just so happened that almost at that exact moment I had detected some movement on the screen just above and to my left. It was about a three foot green mamba. No sooner were the words out of his mouth when I said, *"You mean like that mamba right there."* I never saw a group move so fast en masse. With lightning speed they exited the room. I imagine this story has been told and retold many times by all those who were present.

One night while on the roadway to the hospital the four of us were merrily chatting. Of course I had my ubiquitous AA mini-maglite focused on the road. Suddenly I saw a good sized cobra just in front of us and slightly to my left. Janice was on my left, and in two more steps she'd step on it. I didn't have time to say anything; I just shoved her to the left. Only then did she and the others see what had been imminent. Watchfulness; always watchfulness.

On a much more somber note, most of those who were snake bitten didn't even make it to the hospital. They died in route. Most of the ones who made it to the hospital alive did survive. However, that's not the whole story. Most of the bites were either on the hands or the feet — for obvious reasons. It was fairly common for the venom to cause enough toxic reaction that the area surrounding the bite would become gangrenous (dead tissue) — sometimes the entire hand, arm, foot, or leg. In order to save a person's life it would be necessary to amputate the part involved. This is where it became so sad. In my five years at Chimala I didn't have a single individual who would allow such an amputation. They would choose to leave the hospital in that condition. At this point I think they probably went to a 'native doctor'. I also feel sure that most of them probably died from sepsis (infection throughout their system originating in the gangrenous tissue).

It never failed! Never. There would always be a question about snakes when we were on leave. There seems to be a world wide fascination with these creatures. This question ranked right up there with, "What did you eat?" Once when we were in the USA I gave a talk entitled, "What not to ask a missionary." And you guessed it; I wouldn't be out the door before someone would ask me one of these questions.

"SUFFERING"

"Preach always; if necessary, use words."

– St. Francis of Assisi

This is the title I gave to a Newsletter article dated August 23, 1994. I hadn't been in Africa long before I realized their remarkable response to pain and suffering. I'll let my words from then try to explain:

"How can you talk about suffering? Can you explain so that someone else understands your suffering? Can you understand their suffering? You cannot even feel or totally understand the pain of your closest loved ones. Perhaps you are able if you have had the same problem. But then we forget the pain, don't we? I think this is one of God's most wonderful blessings — being able to forget pain.

We live and work among people where pain, suffering, and death are so very commonplace. They are part of life — so to speak — expected as it were, not just something that happens to someone else. They have seen pain in others; they have experienced pain themselves. As I said, pain is expected — yes, accepted. It does not represent failure or defeat as is often true in the USA.

I see so much suffering, yet words fail me in trying to describe it. Even being away from a particularly bad situation for a few minutes seems to dull my recollection and ability to tell you about it. Why? Is the emotional intensity of the moment lost? Yet I know that in order to be objective as a doctor I must somewhat detach myself — but not too much. I must remain compassionate while retaining clinical effectiveness and emotional control. One of the reasons that Jesus performed miracles was simply that He had compassion. His miracles of healing are well known to you. He was genuinely sorry for peoples' pain and suffering — people like you and me. He often healed people first and then taught them later. Of course He knew that their bodies were temporary and their souls permanent, but His compassion was overpowering and urged Him to heal. He is the Great Physician and my great example.

We currently have a woman at the hospital whose six month old daughter is admitted for pneumonia. She is terribly worried — much more visible than is usual. Why? Her previous seven children have all died! — SUFFERING! — Most of our patients who have major surgery (Caesarean sections, appendectomies, etc.) or have major fractures or severe burns never take narcotics for their pain! Why? Oh yes, we do have some narcotics. On their chart I will order injectable or oral narcotics. The patient will never ask for them, and the nurses will not offer it. Why? Of course they feel pain like you do. They all expect to have pain; they tolerate it. They do not fear pain; it is not their enemy — not something that must be eradicated. Compare this concept to the general approach to pain in the USA. Think about it. How pain is perceived and dealt with is a <u>cultural phenomenon.</u> I have almost forgotten to mention our most common cause of pain — labor and delivery. It is unheard of to have anything for pain at this time.

Can you imagine being taken to the hospital on a bicycle over ten miles of rough road — in shock, with a blood pressure of 60? This particular young woman had amoebic dysentery. SUFFERING! Most of us could not sit up, much less ride on a bicycle in this condition. You would feel extremely weak, sick, sweaty, and faint. The sheer toughness of the Tanzanians never ceases to amaze me.

I am just trying to depict a little bit of what life is like here. Among other things you may realize even more the blessings of your health care opportunities. (You have the "Blessing of Location" and here they are the "Victim of Location"). Yes health care is important. Jesus thought it was — remember. That's why we're here — to improve health care at the same time that we are presenting, teaching, and living Christianity.

Let me just tell you about a not so unusual morning I had last week. Since I was on call, I began my rounds on Obstetrics — our frequent trouble spot. My first two cases were two dead newborns. One was a home delivery where the placenta failed to deliver, and it was too late for the baby. The other baby was born at Chimala after a long labor. The baby was quite depressed due to the amniotic cord being wrapped around the neck. Death occurred shortly after birth. Neither of these would have happened where you live.

[The latter baby may not have died had the midwives called me. Even though we didn't have electronic fetal monitoring, a depressed baby (a baby in difficulty — usually manifested by an extreme slowing of the heart rate) can be detected by a Doppler or by simply listening for the fetal heart with a stethoscope.]

I then went to female ward where one woman was in danger of dying from snake bite. We have no anti-venom here. Another woman was unresponsive from an unknown type of encephalitis. Our testing abilities are most limited. On pediatrics I found two babies in coma — one from cerebral malaria and the other from unknown causes. Another 8 year old was quite confused for unknown reasons (again our laboratory aids and other tests are most limited). A new 14 year old came in with a high fever, confusion, and a stiff neck. A spinal tap proved meningitis. Three newly confirmed cases of AIDS were on male ward this particular morning. During my rounds Margaret came in too late to be helped. She was about 30 and one of our admission clerks. She had severe heart disease for which we could offer so little in our setting.

Are you getting some type of mental picture? I hope so. This Newsletter is rather overwhelming with medical situations. I don't usually do this, and my intention is not for "shock" value or to depress you. These situations and so many more like them encompass our lives here. I think you need to be aware of more of this sometimes.

I remember so well when I wrote this Newsletter. We were in a Guest House on the shore of Lake Malawi near the foot of the mountain leading up to Livingstonia — named after Dr. David Livingstone. Lou Ann and I were on break from the hospital for a few days. The reason I remember it so well was that our monthly letter was due, and I compulsively felt I had to get it done. But the real reason I remember it so well was that my computer was on the blink; and I typed it on a real, honest to goodness typewriter — remember those 'archaic' things. And not just that, it was hot and dark; for surprise, surprise, the electricity was off. Therefore I was using our lantern which attracted every bug in the country of Malawi — at least it seemed that way. So with the poor lighting, a mechanical typewriter without erasing function, the heat, and of course the constantly annoying buzzing, I was able to finish the Newsletter. Memories — memories!

This is an appropriate chapter to talk about "PAIN". All of you have experienced pain, and I must say that you quickly want to know why and then to eradicate the pain. This is normal for our culture. It is NOT that way in the Tanzanian culture. For example, let me tell you about how women handle their labor and delivery. They take NOTHING (yes NOTHING) for the pain. They don't ask for any pain medicine. Why? I think it's because they've seen many deliveries (perhaps had other babies themselves) and pain medicine was not given. They expect it to hurt. And their tolerance is unbelievable. How many of you women have had "natural childbirth" — with no pain medicine and no anesthesia? Very, very few. I'll add that if I order pain medicine for these women, the nurses wouldn't give it. Why? Because pain is expected (everyone has it during labor and delivery), so you will also. This is not a punitive measure nor is it sadistic. It is accepted by all.

During my time at Chimala, we initially had one multi-dose vial of Demerol — a narcotic. Later we did obtain some from the Government Stores. Lou Ann and I were able to procure some Hydrocodone tablets for pain. Once again, these were not used in Obstetrics. We used these meds in post-op patients, severe burns, and fractures. If you know anything about burns, you know that the pain is excruciating. Just imagine the pain of a small blister on your finger and multiply this a 100 times with burns over a large area. (I'll deal more with burns in another chapter).

I continually am totally amazed by the Tanzanians tolerance of pain. Completely the opposite of the USA. When I returned to the USA and worked in Emergency Medicine, there was a uniform concern about pain control ("pain management") by the patients and the nurses. The patients and their families expected any pain to be alleviated — and quickly. As care givers, we were judged by our sensitivity and response to pain. This public attitude and more have helped lead to our 'epidemic' of pain medicine abuse and addiction.

STORY OF THE MILK

"Acts without words are meaningless; words without acts have no credibility."

E arly in my time at Chimala I began to go over the hospital expenses. One unusual expense item I noticed was the cost of milk which was given daily to the men who took X-rays. Upon speaking to Ezekiel, our chief X-ray "technician", he said that milk protected them from any damages caused by X-rays. I had never heard of such a thing and knew it was fallacious. As I discussed it with Ezekiel, I could tell he wasn't accepting my explanation. He didn't know who had started using the milk, but it was a habit that been perpetuated for many years. I didn't want to berate him or make him feel foolish, so I told him that we would discuss it later.

This was not a matter of the money. I just wanted to educate and correct their misunderstanding. I found a medical article dealing with how to be protected from the damages of X-ray. Since milk wasn't mentioned in the article, Ezekiel took this to mean that milk was still a factor in protection. Our discussion went on intermittently for several months.

Finally I found the answer! Or so I thought. It came to my attention I could get radiation badges that determined how much radiation exposure occurred over a given period of time. I would then send them off to be read at the determined intervals. When the first reading returned quite low and well within the safe level, I shared this with Ezekiel. At that point I told him this was proof that there was no danger from our X-ray machine. I don't think he was convinced. However, at this point I did take away the daily milk.

What I haven't mentioned was the fact that we took very few X-rays — some days none at all. This in itself was actually sufficient enough reason not to be concerned. I did continue sending off the badges at regular intervals. They were never even close to the danger zone. I did find out later that Ezekiel's major concern was the possibility of sterility with excess exposure.

Lou Ann's Jobs

*"The words of Jesus, "Love one another as I have loved you",
must not only be a light for us but a flame that consumes the self in us......
Love, to be real, must cost — it must hurt — it must be nourished
by sacrifice, especially the sacrifice of self."*

–Mother Teresa

What did Lou Ann do? That's easy. Everything but the practice of medicine. She took care of all the ancillary needs to support the medical work. You cannot do proper medical work without the medicines and the necessary supplies. Organization and efficiency, which were direly needed, were provided by Lou Ann. From the storerooms to the pharmacy to the cleaners, she provided the leadership.

When we first arrived, the staff didn't really know what supplies were available. Many items had been shipped from the USA via container but hadn't been properly labeled and stored in an organized fashion. If you don't know you have something or what it's for, you might as well not have it. To go through all the storerooms and properly label and organize was a huge task. She became the authority on what we had (or didn't have) and just as important — where it was. If I needed something and no one seemed to know, I'd say, "Go get Lou Ann!"

She also directed the pharmacy and the pharmacy staff. This was no small task — keeping up with the medicines, how much we had, what we needed, where to get it, the cost, the inventory, and "a partridge in a pear tree". I've mentioned that she scoured the world in trying to get the medicines we needed. Some were available in the Tanzanian Government Stores, but their formulary was limited and unpredictable. She also got medicines from England, Holland, India, Kenya, South Africa, the USA; and I'm sure I've left out some places. I have no doubt that we eventually had the most complete pharmacy in the country. It was rather common for patients or their families to come from other medical facilities to obtain medicines and supplies from us. If we had an adequate supply, we tried to help them.

A regular inventory and a double check system were necessary in order to curtail pilfering (stealing) medicines and supplies. This took a lot of valuable time but just had to be done. I well remember those monthly inventories when Lou Ann had Janice and me help count (yes count) every pill in the pharmacy to make sure the number matched the books. Yuck! A laborious, necessary task.

She directed the cleaning ladies at the hospital. One of my favorite memories was how Lou Ann introduced the use of mops and mop buckets to clean the hospital floors. The way the cleaning ladies had always cleaned the floors was with old rags. They would put soapy water on the floor, steadily walk backward while bending at the waist, and scrubbing as they went. Oooh my back! Lou Ann became the "mop lady".

Shopping; oh, I can't forget her shopping. Once per week she would drive the two hour round trip to Mbeya (our closest town with "stores" and our referral government hospital). This was definitely not your routine trip to Krogers. It took her all day. My only "rules" were that she couldn't go alone and no live animals in our Land Cruiser. By the way, this didn't include animals on the top rack. Chickens and goats found their transportation there. John went with her each week. He had been hired to help Lou Ann at the hospital and at our house. (John followed Earnest as our second "yard man"). About 9AM each Tuesday Lou Ann and John and an uncertain number of others would pile in our vehicle and head out — usually not returning until 5PM. She would make numerous stops at various maduka (shops) to buy groceries, supplies, and whatever other items for all the missionaries on the compound. I'm making this sound simplistic and quick, but of course it wasn't. John always tried to make sure we got the proper Tanzanian price and not the "wazungu price" (white person). Besides shopping with many merchants in the market place, she would take blood samples to the Government Hospital and pick up the results from the previous week. Upon her return to Chimala, our vehicle reminded me of the Beverly Hillbillies — crammed full of everything imaginable with the top rack stacked to the max.

Even though she didn't carry animals inside the Land Cruiser, she often carried "chicken food" — ground corn plus whatever. One of our nurses raised chickens for some extra money. The reason I'm telling you this is to explain what this brought about. We often left our vehicle at the Swedish Free Mission in Dar es Salaam when we went to the USA on furlough. Due to the leakage from the "chicken food" sacks, rats found our vehicle a very convenient place to occupy and feast. You can imagine their too numerous droppings throughout. But worse than this were the holes they had eaten in the upholstery.

Lou Ann also directed our house workers. Rehema came five days per week to clean the house and wash clothes, do some local marketing, plus whatever other tasks Lou Ann assigned. Rehema probably stood about four foot nothing. She was a fair cleaner at best, but I jokingly told Lou Ann that I didn't think Rehema ever looked up. What I mean is that various critters and their webs were routinely on the walls, ceiling, and fans — above her line of sight.

She also had John take care of the yard work, our many flowers, and small garden. He was quite meticulous, and we had the most and prettiest flowers on the compound. Some of this is due to Lou Ann confiscating cuttings from anywhere and everywhere. Regarding our small garden I should tell you the story of the jalapeno peppers. Even though there were many peppers in Tanzania, we couldn't find jalapenos. Since we like them so much, we brought seeds from the USA. With our warmer climate and John's regular watering we had bumper crops of jalapenos year round. Tanzanians really liked them, so we supplied a host of folks.

Zebron was our cook. What a fine, sweet older man he was! He had cooked for the British as a young man before Tanzanian independence. He spoke no English but could figure out any recipe Lou Ann had. She taught him to make bagels, and fine ones they were — probably the only bagels in Tanzania. Needless to say; because Zebron was an excellent cook, we ate quite well. And oh my; those pies! I can still taste them.

In addition to her fine Christian example she regularly taught a ladies Bible class at church — all in Swahili of course. Quite a challenge! I remember her telling me about one of the initial classes when everyone introduced themselves. Two of the older ladies in the class had had eleven children between them — and none of their children were alive. Another tragic example of the harshness of the area in which we serve.

A task that was probably less to Lou Ann's liking was that of keeping me in line. Not an easy chore. I talk more about her support in the chapter, "*Sources of Strength.*" I must say that she tolerated the overriding inefficiency and lack of variety much better than I did. She also did much better with Swahili. Frankly, I was envious; but I was proud of her language usage and ability to handle all her tasks well (I'm sure I've left out some). I truthfully said many times that the Tanzanians would miss Mama Blacki more than yours truly when we left Chimala.

Tragic Obstetric Death

"When someone you love needs medical help fast, your perspective changes. Suddenly your world is reduced to one objective: Help them survive. Americans are used to hospitals minutes away, doctors and nurses on duty, lifesaving procedures, with the latest technology and medication available. — When you live in a developing country, all bets are off."

— Kay Warren

This is the story of Ester Zabron. When she came to our hospital, it had been eighteen months since our last obstetric death. We were very proud of this fact. It takes much attention to the women — their progress in labor, their vital signs, and their recovery after delivering. It's frankly a lot of work and literally is a 24/7 job every day. Unlike the USA, obstetrical deaths are all too common in developing countries. This is especially true when women deliver in their villages. If they come to a hospital with midwives and doctors, both mothers and their babies will do so much better.

It was 2:30 in the afternoon just after Ester had delivered her baby. This was her fourth baby from five pregnancies (one child had died). After her delivery by one of our midwives, she kept having heavy vaginal bleeding. Usually after delivery of the baby and the placenta, the uterus contracts quickly and bleeding is minimal. Since the bleeding continued to be heavy, the midwife suspected some tearing and called me to evaluate her situation. Indeed on examination she had sustained some severe cervical and vaginal tears. (The cervix is the outlet portion of the uterus.). Tears are usually caused by a delivery that is too abrupt, a very large baby, or some manipulation by the midwife or doctor that is too vigorous. Tears are sometimes unavoidable.

In such situations with tearing the bleeding is quite severe because there is still much blood flow into the woman's pelvic organs, having just sustained a baby. You can just imagine how difficult and messy such a situation is. A woman can bleed to death in a matter of minutes. So I began acting quickly. Start IV fluids, send blood for type and cross match for possible transfusion, get an anesthetic ready (repair is usually done while the woman is asleep — very painful), have a good light source, good suction, an assistant, the proper surgical instruments and suture, a steady hand, and lots of patience. You can already see why this procedure is quite difficult. It is one of the hardest procedures I did at Chimala — more difficult by far than doing a C-section. I hope this doesn't bother you; but when you're looking in a vagina that's just delivered a baby, it's bloody, dark, and distorted. The tissue is thin, easily torn, and bleeding like crazy. You can see why a good light source and good suction are needed. It's difficult and most important to make sure you sew the right part to the right part. I'm not trying to be funny — just being honest about it. In this new post-delivery situation all the tissue can look remarkably similar. First of all I want to control the emergency situation (bleeding and shock), but at the same time get a good repair. This is quite necessary, for she'll want more babies. You want her to have a properly functioning uterus and birth canal. Do you begin to see not only the difficulty of this repair but its implications?

I'll spare you more details here. I finished repairing Ester's tears, and the bleeding seemed to be under control. The midwife was to watch her closely and have the lab give her a transfusion. As I finished, another nurse wanted me to check a new OB case. This was a young lady with her first baby. She had what we call CPD (cephalopelvic disproportion). This is simply when the baby's head is too big for the mother's pelvis. In addition the baby was in distress — as manifested by a slowing heart rate. Off we went to do a C-section. Things went smoothly, and mother and baby did well.

It was 4PM when I completed the C/S and headed to OB to check on Ester. I found her lying in bed — dead! The nurse didn't even know it yet. I can't tell you how I felt — how sad, how appalled, even guilty. Why? Oh why did she die? My immediate thought was, "Oh no; she's bled out right here under their noses." But upon further examination there was little evidence of continued bleeding. What happened? Certainly her death was from blood loss and shock. To my further dismay I discovered that she had not gotten the transfusion I'd ordered. The blood for her was still in the lab refrigerator.

A preventable death? Yes. Terrible doesn't even begin to tell you how badly I felt. Of course I felt partially responsible. I tried to investigate the course of events that transpired from the time I last saw her. Just where did things break down? As usual in such matters, my investigation came to a quick conclusion. The Nursing Supervisor's determination was that there was no fault. No disciplinary action was incurred. My plea to our staff and my prayer was that this would never happen again.

While I'm writing about very sad and disastrous cases, I'll add one more. This case was just as sad but in a different way. You'll only see such cases in a developing country where there's the culmination of so many factors — many babies, minimal to no pre-natal care, poor health before pregnancy, limited education regarding their bodies, little available medical care, poor transportation, reliance on self designated village "mid-wives", and the list goes on and on.......

Tulia Sanga was a young woman with her first pregnancy. Just like you ladies she would have had all the expectations of her child's birth. In her culture she would be "fulfilling her role". She would have been the center of attention for the other ladies in her village. It was a joyous time for her. When she went into labor, she did what the majority of women in her village did — she went to a local "birther". Most such women had enough experience, however, to know when labor was not progressing properly and would refer them to our hospital. In this sense we had somewhat of a "screened population" of patients who often required C-sections. But unfortunately this decision was made much too late in

Tulia's case. When she came to us, the baby had been in the vagina for three days (an hour is too long for a baby to be in this position). Of course the baby was dead. Not only this, but infection had set in. And to make the situation even worse, it was apparent that some of her vagina and cervix were necrotic (dead tissue). It was a horrible situation. In order to try and save her life, she needed to have a hysterectomy (removal of the uterus). She would not consent to this. Why not? You know the answer. She wanted more babies. It was not unusual for men to leave their wives if they were unable to bear children.

I removed the dead baby and put her on IV antibiotics while continuing to try and talk her into surgery. The next day she agreed. In the interim she had probably spoken to her husband. The women almost always acquiesced to their husbands' decision. Fortunately, Dr. Dean Paulson (an Ob-Gyn doctor) was present. At surgery much of the uterus and a portion of the vagina were necrotic. We removed as much dead tissue as possible, but it seemed like an impossible situation. In her condition I don't think her chances would have been good even in the best American referral center. She died two days later from sepsis (overwhelming infection). — Such a tragic and preventable situation — another example of being a victim of location.

CULTURAL "TIDBITS" AND MORE

"Everything in life can make us either better or bitter."

So many incidents and observations are experienced when you live in a totally different culture. They can be happy or sad; they're not right or wrong; not good or bad; just different. In this chapter I'll relate some of the many we had the pleasure of learning and experiencing.

- "It's but a dream."
  Our hospital administrator, Bernard Kulanga, has a Master's Degree. Besides the medical doctors, he was the most educated person on our staff. His salary, even though it met Government standards, was rather meager. When we spoke of his having a car, he said, *"It's but a dream."* Anyone who owned a car was considered rich. And we missionaries 'fit that bill'. Some of the Tanzanians thought that we must be making a lot of money at the hospital. Consequently, I made it a point occasionally to tell them that all our monetary support came from donors in the USA. (I hope they believed me).

- Time is not linear [or progressive] as we tell time:
  Time is just not that important. Time is more *event oriented*. It's the event that matters and not the time or date. Consequently, most Tanzanians do not know the date of their birth nor how old they are. They might say they were born during planting season. By the way, the expression, *"How old are you?"*, doesn't make sense to the Tanzanians. They would ask, *"How many years do you have?"*. Speaking of time; some experienced missionaries say one of the best things to do is NOT to wear a watch. I could never do that.

- Where are you from?

  Just like you can tell if someone's from the deep South or Boston,
  Tanzanians can tell within 100 miles what part of Tanzania
  someone is from. Don't worry; no one ever accused me of this
  talent. I was too busy trying to decipher whether they had told
  me "yes" or "no". As I've stated, my poor Swahili skills were a
  constant impediment and embarrassment.

- Discrimination — What do you think?

  I mentioned our hospital administrator. He had traveled over
  various parts of Tanzania in connection with his work. (Later he
  even went to the USA). His wife, Lida, worked with my wife in
  the Storeroom. Lou Ann found out that Lida had never been to
  Mbeya — our nearest city and only 50 miles away. Actually Lou
  Ann went there once weekly for shopping and other duties.
  Well, you can easily guess who was on Lou Ann's next shopping
  trip! Lida of course. You ladies are probably appalled. This is
  just the way it is. It was not considered to be restrictive or punitive or discriminatory. And yes, it was accepted by women as the
  way things were — the norm. This is yet another example of the
  African culture being definitely a male dominant culture.

  An interesting sidelight about the trip to Mbeya. Since many of
  the Tanzanians had never ridden in a vehicle on the curvy roads,
  it was not unusual for them to succumb to severe motion sickness — much like little children do.

- Travel paraphernalia:

  On our trips to Dar es Salaam (the Capitol city some 500 miles
  from Chimala) we would have our coolers, extra water, food, a
  couple of suit cases, etc. When we took our Tanzanian friends
  with us, they would show up with perhaps one medium-sized
  plastic bag with all their items. You're ahead of me. Yes, we felt
  extravagant and embarrassed. All our 'stuff'. Most of ours was
  unnecessary. This more accurately depicted our excess rather
  than their deficiency.

- Items sent from the USA:

  It's really amazing what would be placed on the containers we received from the USA. Of course we received many excellent items, but some of the supplies were rather unbelievable. It became clear that no one went through the items stateside. Of course this would be a huge job. Do you realize how big a 40 foot container is? It can easily hold a couple cars and more.

  How about a pair of scissors with an attached tag saying, *"Broken"*. And then there are the coloring books — already colored! And along with them were the one inch long crayons and pencils. What about medical machines that not only didn't work but were so old that spare parts couldn't be obtained anywhere (and remember, this is Africa where the machines had never been used). We adopted the phrase, *"If it's broken in America, it's broken in Africa."*

- Positive or Negative:

  If I said to you, *"You don't have a car do you?"* You would quickly answer, "No" (meaning: *"No; I don't have a car"*). Swahili speakers would answer the question by saying, *"Yes"*. Follow me now; they are saying, *"Yes, we don't have a car."* This is the reverse of how we speak and more than a little confusing at first.

- "African Speed Bumps":

  Once when we were merrily tooling along on a narrow shaded road near the top of the Ngorongoro Crater, our heads were suddenly thrown against the roof of our Land Cruiser. What happened!? As we put it together, we realized we had hit what looked like a speed bump. Yes, a speed bump. I slowed considerably and became much more observant. Sure enough another of these too tall mounds appeared across the road. There were a series of them. Why? There were no houses visible, no cross roads, no road signs. In fact, we didn't pass another vehicle in the area. Someone of 'authority' had become too enamored with speed bumps. I think they missed the lecture on where to place them.

- African Pillows:
We've stayed at a number of Guest Houses, Motels, and Hotels when traveling around various countries in Africa. It seemed that the pillows everywhere were quite consistent in that they were hard as stone. It was ubiquitous. They were basically unusable — unless you wanted to awaken with a stiff neck and a severe headache. When possible we began carrying our own pillows. I now know that it's a proven scientific fact: African foam turns to concrete over time. Yes it does.

- The Burning Mountain:
Not far behind our house in Chimala the mountains began to rise abruptly. They were quite steep and rugged, rendering the land unusable to farm. Every year near the end of dry season the sides of the mountain would be ablaze. The standard of farming was to slash and burn before the rains came. But remember; no one farmed the mountains nor lived there. So who started the fires remained a mystery. And the bigger question was, "Why?" I asked several Tanzanians and never got a consistent answer. The best answer I ever received was, *"They burn it so that next year people can say — Remember that fire on the mountain last year?"*

- "Do you have a ....?":
You can fill in the blank. If you ask an African this question, the answer will usually come back, *"Oh yes, we have one."* We found out by experience that our follow-up question should be, *"Does it work?"* And you should then consider the question, *"When was the last time it worked?"*

Like I said; we learned through experience. On one occasion as we were checking into a hotel, I asked, *"Does the room have an air conditioner?"* *"Oh yes, most certainly"*, came the reply. We did stay there. The room indeed had an A/C unit, but an inspection quickly showed it probably hadn't worked in years. I should add that this particular experience occurred early in our sojourn in Tanzania. We learned quickly.

Once as I was visiting our referral hospital in Mbeya, I saw an ultrasound machine in the X-ray department. I said, *"I see you have an ultrasound machine!"* *"Oh yes; a very nice one."* Then I asked my follow-up question, *"When was the last time you used it?"* The answer came back *"Six months ago."* It turned out that they had no ultrasound gel and were awaiting some from the German company that had given them the machine. (This sentiment alone tells quite a story about 'dependence'). Actually I made my own gel for our Doppler when we couldn't get "official gel."

- Operating room hazards:

I've mentioned the cascading sweat in the OR elsewhere. Another hazard was yours truly getting blisters (yes blisters) on my thumbs from old, donated, stiff hemostats and needle holders. They had been discarded in the USA and sent to us. AMAZING, yet it happened on a number of occasions. I've had to stop surgery to have an assistant pull up my scrub pants that had decided to descend to my knees. This was the result of the string tie being broken. You guessed it; sent from the USA.

An ancillary function of our anesthetist was to shoo flies and other flying or crawling varmints from the operative field. And yes, I've had to pick bugs from inside someone's belly. Sweat, bugs, other! Our patients seemed extremely tough and resistant to infection from these unwanted sources. Kind of gross though, huh!

We had a fancy looking overhead surgical light — one problem; it wouldn't focus on one spot. The light was too diffuse. For my focused lighting I used a light that stands on the floor — one problem; it had a mind of its own and "drifted" out of position, requiring someone to constantly hold it in position. Why was it discarded and sent from the USA. You guessed it. Because it drifted.

I must tell you about our back-up surgical lighting system. The lights I mentioned above were all electrically powered. They depended on either National Power or our local generator. With frequent power outages and about fifteen minutes needed to switch over to the generator, you can see a huge problem — especially at night. And now my "special back-up lighting system" would be used a <u>D-cell Maglight.</u> It sufficed quite nicely and was used on several occasions. I would have a designated person to 'man the light' immediately if we lost electrical power.

One more hazard in the OR, and this time I do mean a very dangerous hazard. I'm talking about the use of ether as an anesthetic. It is a decent anesthetic with one major drawback—it's explosive! (I'll add here that my grandfather, Dr. William Black, used ether in the 1920's and 30's.). Ether has been outdated for over 50 years, yet Chimala had an ether machine. One huge problem. It had a leak and the distinctive odor of ether quickly filled the room. Remember that ether is readily explosive and potentially could wipe out everyone in the room. Upon my first arriving at Chimala and scrubbing in with the Tanzanian doctors, I was appalled with their use of ether and the defective machine. The main danger was obvious (an explosion), but on a personal level the escaping ether gave me nausea and a dreadful headache. Being the new "Doctor in Charge" (Mganga Mkuu) I quickly made my first executive decision — REMOVE THE ETHER MACHINE; WE'RE NOT USING IT ANYMORE.

- <u>Bride Price:</u>
  You probably know what this is. It's when a male suitor wants a certain young lady to be his bride. He must approach the lady's father and bargain (yes bargain) for her. The arrived upon amount can be paid in money, goods, animals, etc. This practice is in the Old Testament. You may remember Jacob eventually working 14 years for Rachel. This was indeed true love. How many of you guys would do that? Don't answer out loud. The practice is still quite prevalent in Tanzania — even though it is diminishing among those with higher education. One of our more highly trained nurses, Augustino Mbunda, recently got married. The bride price he paid to his father-in-law was one

cow, two goats, two blankets, five kanga (pieces of cloth), and 50,000 Tanzanian shillings (about $83.00) — pretty amazing and yet rather standard amounts.

This practice does hark back to the idea that women are property; and therefore, they must be bought. The husband then owns his wife. This is current reality in many places, even though I know it will be repulsive to many of you.

- "Do their knees bend?" and "Story of the Mops":
  You would quickly notice what we did — that most Africans bend at the waist and not with their knees. I'm talking about when they pick up both small and heavy loads from ground level. (We're taught to "bend your knees" when lifting in order to spare your back). When women are bathing their children in a tub on the ground they bend over at the waist from a standing position. A short-handled hoe is used hour after hour as they work on their farms — forcing them to bend at the waist. What really got me was watching the cleaning ladies at the hospital. I told about this in *"Lou Ann's Jobs"*. What I didn't say was that when the mops were used up, they immediately reverted to their former way without complaining. This seemed to be a truism of Africans — when something is used up or broken, they just accept it and proceed in their former way as if nothing had happened. This is an amazing quality.

- African "Efficiency" — An Oxymoron: (see Chapter on "Patience and Efficiency")
  In the USA efficiency is just taken for granted. It is basically ingrained and expected from our very beginning. A premium is put on efficiency in every phase of our lives — the easiest, best, and quickest way of doing things. But efficiency is not a factor of intelligence; it is learned. When in Africa, you quickly observe that the way things are done is often far from being the most efficient way. It just seems that they don't think from the standpoint

of 'how to do it more efficiently'. Perhaps it's because 'things were always done this way' or 'someone set it up this way'. I imagine it's also tied in with their view of time. *What's the hurry?"* In fact, a Swahili proverb says, *"Haraka, haraka; haina baraka."* This says, *"Hurry, hurry; it has no blessing."* The Swahili word for white man is *Mzungu.* The base for this word is a verb meaning "to go around and around". As the story goes, the first Europeans were called *'mzungu'* because they were always busy running around and around. "If the shoe fits............"

I've always worked on being as efficient as possible and admit I had some pride in this. It was a good quality to have in my career as an Emergency Physician in the USA. What I'm leading up to was that the lack of efficiency drove me crazy! Just ask Lou Ann. I struggled to teach our hospital employees to become more efficient. I lost the battle. In order to keep my sanity, I just worked on being as efficient as I personally could. I couldn't impose it on others.

I probably went 'over the top' in trying to be efficient. Here's an example: This relates to how I did spinal taps (lumbar punctures). We frequently had outbreaks of meningitis, and we always had seizures from malaria. This necessitated my doing spinal taps to differentiate the two. Believe it or not; I had EVERYTHING in my medical bag that was required to do the procedure. This was so that I could do it quickly and not have to scurry around gathering the needed supplies — or even slower to have someone else scurry for me. Here's what I had in my bag:

- Sterile gloves
- Alcohol wipes to clean the skin
- Sterile gauze
- Syringes with needles for xylocaine
- Xylocaine for local anesthesia
- Spinal needles for children and adults
- Tubes for collection of spinal fluid
- Bandaids to cover the puncture site

I did the procedures at the patient's bedside during rounds in a matter of minutes. You can see this was most efficient. Let me tell you one more thing. Instead of sending the spinal fluid to the lab for determination, I used the "frankus blackus clarity test". I'm not trying to be facetious; but if the fluid is even the least bit cloudy, that is a positive test for bacterial meningitis. (Malaria, seizures, and viral meningitis don't cause cloudy fluid). In being more medically sophisticated, there are usually more than 200 white blood cells per high power field under the microscope in bacterial meningitis. And at this level of white blood cells the spinal fluid just begins to look very faintly cloudy — thus the 'clarity test'. I usually did send the fluid to the lab for what we call a Gram Stain — this helps determine what type bacteria is causing the meningitis. But since we treated all bacterial types with the same antibiotic, this test was a moot point. Don't tell your local doctors my secret method.

While I'm at it; I'll tell you more about a tremendous source of curiosity among the Tanzanians. I'm speaking again about my bag — that green Land's End bag I had with me all the time and I mean all the time. In addition to the supplies needed for the spinal taps, I had a seemingly infinite supply of other medical equipment for whatever occasion arose. This way I was sure to have what I needed with me — no running around and looking (remember; efficiency!). I never got so many stares as when I delved into my magic bag and pulled out whatever. It was like Aladdin's lamp — what would come forth next?

Related to efficiency is planning ahead. To restock something before it runs out seems fairly simple and important — right! This was another concept Lou Ann and I struggled with our entire five years. Were we successful? Only sometimes with some people. Let me give you an example. Initially we took X-rays twice a week in the evening. On a day when X-rays were to be taken I found only a few plates in the department. Why? Ephraim had used most of them the last time. Had he asked for more? No. Did he know he was about out? Yes. Why? We could have fairly easily gotten more plates. This is the frustrating part. It's part of the cultural mind set — so difficult to comprehend and so difficult to change.

- <u>Tanzanian Construction:</u>
  In our First World of convenience and often too much of everything, we assume certain things. How about mirrors in the bathroom for example. What if you don't have a bathroom? Then you would never think of putting a mirror in a bathroom you're building. When they are put in, they're often put in the wrong place. Often they're too low. Why? They're put in to fit the shorter workers.

  And then there are the plug outlets. We have our electrical codes in the USA, but what of those who don't have electricity? They have no idea where the outlets should be placed. Once again; the outlets are either not present or are in awkward places. One of my favorites has to do with the placement of a light switch — which our workers didn't have in their houses. We added a storage room behind our house — of course with a light switch. Guess where the switch was? It was behind the door. In other words you had to open the door, go inside, and reach behind the door to turn on the light. Awkward? Yes. But more than that — the room was known to house rats and snakes. I didn't want to risk turning on the misplaced switch, so I always approached the room with my flashlight in hand.

  We all have bars for hanging clothes in our closets. These bars are usually placed so that we can easily place a hanger on them. Not the bar we had at Chimala. It was placed quite close to the shelf above it, making the placement of hangers most difficult. So what do you expect when the workers had no idea of how to use it.

For the sake of using the minimal amount of cloth I presume, our workers put curtains up with the exact measurements of the space needed. As you know, curtains are made with a scalloped or pleated pattern, so as to properly cover the window. Therefore, we were constantly yanking on the curtains to cover the windows at night (until Lou Ann had some more made). The same philosophy must have been used in mosquito net making. They were never quite big enough.

These seem like simple things to you; but if you have no experience with something, you just don't know. As I always say, it's ignorance of the situation but not stupidity. We are all ignorant in some areas.

- Where are all the people?"
  In Tanzania the people basically are up and busy from sun up to sun down. They are outside their homes making fires, cooking, getting water, carrying wood for the fire, getting ready for market, children playing, people talking, etc. This is every day — seven days a week. Compare this to your American neighborhood. Most mornings you see no one outside — perhaps a single car leaving a closed garage and headed to work. On Sundays you won't even see this. In America we 'cocoon' ourselves; we have everything we need in our homes; we don't need to be outside our temperature regulated homes to be social. We have our various devices of media and social communication. One recent Sunday I must have passed fifty homes on the way to church and saw no sign of human life — none. Amazing difference in our cultures. Now you tell me which one is better.

- Liquids do run uphill:
  We all learned in science class that one of the definitions of a liquid is that it runs downhill. I found an exception to that law of physics. The exception is mother's milk. What am I talking

about? Many times we witnessed a suckling child wrapped comfortably on mother's back as the breast was pulled as far as possible up toward the shoulder and within reach of the child's eager mouth (get the picture?). The child always seemed satisfied with the milk that ran uphill.

Another observation here about mother's breast milk. It was the 'great tranquilizer' for babies in Tanzania. I don't believe I ever saw what we call a 'pacifier' in the USA that's plugged into babies' mouths and functions as a "tranquilizer". The Tanzanian way works quite well; and besides, the "tranquilizer" never gets lost.

Believe it or not; the female breast is not an object of sexual desire in Tanzania. Coming from our breast-oriented American culture, complete with augmentation, cleavage, and advertisements; I think men and women alike have difficulty realizing this. But it is entirely true. Breasts serve their God-given function of being their babies' food source. Because of this, women's modesty has nothing to do with covering their breasts. In our hot environment they frequently didn't cover.

Humorous things do occur in relation to this. It's interesting to watch our male (and female) newcomers and their response. Perhaps feeling uncomfortable, somewhat embarrassed, and not knowing where to look, they try to look nonchalant. My father-in-law visited us, and his comments were novel. He said, *"I've never seen a situation where a woman starts taking off their clothes when a man walks up."* He was referring to the women preparing for me to see them on rounds.

- Public Displays:
Tanzanians show no public display of affection. I'm referring to male/female behavior. In fact, husbands almost would not even acknowledge their wives in public. The wife would walk behind her husband. I think this is holdover from a male dominant culture. I know USA women find this reprehensible. Contrariwise, men would hold another man's hand and women another

woman's hand. This was a sign of friendship — no sexual overtones. I readily admit my discomfort with this practice. Lou Ann
gleefully would tell you about my expression when Dr. Badi (one
of our Tanzanian doctors) reached out and held my hand as we
walked at the hospital. I really tried to hide my hesitance and
embarrassment.

Every culture has various hand and other gestures. They key here
is, "If in doubt, don't use them." In Tanzania the left hand is the
"bathroom hand." Consequently, the left hand should not be
offered to shake hands or accept items. This was quite difficult
for me, for I'm a lefty. Pointing with the forefinger is also not
appropriate. Tanzanians move their head or mouth to denote a
person or direction. I never quite got this down either. I've only
scratched the surface regarding various behaviors or gestures.
Just think how many we have in the USA.

WHAT IS THIRD WORLD MEDICINE?

can't improve on the definition of "Third World Medicine" I wrote in
a Newsletter:

*"Third World Medicine is where you have the highest volume of the sick-
est patients with the most delayed presentations and the most bizarre diagnoses
arriving by the most perilous transportation and seeing the fewest and least
trained medical personnel. Add in the least medical equipment and tests, insuf-
ficient support personnel, and the least medications. Also factor in the remote
tropical culture where inefficiency is the standard; the miniscule knowledge
patients have of their bodies and disease; the "competition" is the local witch
doctor; and pain and death are resolutely accepted."* — Now you are beginning to understand.

This next section is also taken directly from a Newsletter and more
vividly depicts the answer to this Chapter's question:

*"I am sitting here peacefully writing, listening to a gentle rain on our tin
roof, and listening to some soothing Indian flute music on our tape player. It
is quiet. I am alone. Lou Ann has gone with Janice and Beth to a Christian
Women's Retreat in Meru, Kenya. But Africa is a land of contrasts — never
ending contrasts. I am on call and have just returned from my night rounds. I
just admitted two small infants and left them fighting for their lives — not to
mention so many other patients with severe illnesses. One child is eight months
old and desperately anemic from malaria. There are just not enough red blood
cells left to carry sufficient oxygen, so she is quite short of breath and too weak
to eat. A transfusion is lifesaving for children like this. Oxygen is most helpful, but at this time we had none. The other child has severe pneumonia and
likewise needs oxygen. Contrast your medical concerns in the USA with these
two cases — plus my other patients with tuberculosis, tetanus, typhoid fever,*

yaws, amoebic liver abscess, fractured femur (in traction for six weeks), relapsing fever, severe malnutrition, glomerulonephritis, three ladies with end stage cervical cancer (due to no Pap smears). I think I'd better quit, but this is only a partial rundown of my current patients. This is probably too much for you non-medical people to comprehend, and you're probably scurrying around to "Google" the diseases.

I don't want to overwhelm you. I just want to help depict how most of the third world lives. It is real. These are real, caring, suffering people who love their families as much as you do. This is their life. Most health care facts that you have known since elementary school are not known to them. Combine this with filth, poverty, lack of availability of health care, lack of transportation; and this results in the types of patients I've described. Sure they live with much pain and suffering and death; but they are a vibrant, tough, yet gentle people. Their harsh lives actually make it easier for them to understand and accept the truth of Christianity than for people in the USA. [This depicts well why I am here — to help medically and spiritually.]

Please remember this the next time you are tempted to complain about or hear someone complain about the health care system you have (imperfect though it may be). Also think about the child I had who was bitten by a rabid dog when there is no available anti-rabies vaccine. And the women with the worst hand infection I've ever seen who had walked two days to get to Chimala. I drained a basin full of pus from her hand. Think of the woman who was carried on a litter down the mountain behind us. (This is a several hour climb walking alone and with good hiking boots.). She had a perforated gastric (stomach) ulcer and died post-operatively from severe peritonitis. It had just been too long. It goes without saying that knowledge, availability, proper communication, and transportation would have saved this woman. I shared the grief with all six of her children who helped carry her down the mountain."

Many chapters in my book deal with various aspects of patients and their maladies. These help give a more comprehensive picture of Third World medicine. Having said this, there are certain quite distinguishing characteristics of medicine in a "bush hospital" in a developing country.

These would become readily apparent to any medical person who has also worked in current Western medicine. Several hallmarks are listed, but I deal with them more completely in other chapters:

- Delayed presentation (advanced disease):

    This is without doubt the most common factor in defining, "What is Third World Medicine?" — even more than the various tropical diseases. In the USA we see diseases most commonly in their early stages. Absolutely not so in Tanzania! Seeing some common wound or disease in its early stages is an entirely different entity than when presenting late (sometimes hardly recognizable). Delayed presentation is a combination of several factors: lack of patient knowledge of medicine and disease; lack of transportation; lack of medical facilities; lack of money; innate stoicism and plain old toughness; other cultural factors. You just name the disease, and I saw it in an advanced stage. Things you would never see in the USA — only read about. At the advanced stage of diseases they are much more difficult to treat and are often very poorly responsive — if at all.

- Tropical Diseases:

    It's obvious that in the tropics we saw a myriad of tropical diseases. No surprise here. This is an area I had to especially study up on before moving to Tanzania, because these diseases are virtually never seen in the USA. I had my books and pictures on Tropical Medicine; but having never seen the diseases, I got a lot of OJT [on the job training] from our medical staff at Chimala (see one; diagnose one). I won't go into any discussion here of the various diseases. I will mention two of the more common entities: intestinal parasites (worms) and the ubiquitous malaria. Worms were so common that the treatment was generally given to everyone. They cause abdominal pain, malnutrition, anemia, and worse. Virtually everyone had malaria — meaning they had it chronically with acute flare-ups 2-3 times per year. Malaria along with HIV/AIDS caused most our deaths. It was quite hard on little children and was their number one cause of death. I speak of cerebral malaria elsewhere — this is the most severe type of malaria and unfortunately the common type in Chimala.

- "Pus":

I'm not trying to gross you out or trying to be funny. It's quite true. What do I mean? With delayed presentation of boils (abscesses), believe me they can get huge. You name the area of the body, and they occur there. There are so many abscesses because of their very unsanitary living conditions, resulting very dirty skin, infrequent washing, plus the delayed presentation. What's the treatment of an abscess? Simple. It's drainage. I'm not exaggerating when I tell you I've gotten a pint of pus from various abscesses. Repeated cleaning and drainage, debridement of dead tissue, antibiotics, and time — time. This is the treatment. I don't want to gross you out more, but here goes. I could usually tell what type of bacteria caused the abscess by the odor. True. Some are quite foul — nauseatingly foul. I won't be any more descriptive.

- HIV/AIDS:

Sub-Saharan Africa is well known as the epicenter of HIV/AIDS. All the world statistics show that the prevalence is greatest here. In Tanzania we were in that area. I can't say enough how devastating it is — absolutely devastating. My chapter on HIV/AIDS goes into detail.

- Pain and Death:

Because of all the factors I've discussed, the natural course of events leads to pain (suffering) and death. It's so sad; we just carry on and do the best we can in our setting. We don't want to become calloused or inured to the pain and death. This can happen. The solemn faces and stoicism of Tanzanians can appear to show acceptance — even passivity. This is deceptive, for this is the mode they have to adopt when so much pain and death have been witnessed. We always caution our students about witnessing death — many of them have never had a patient die (especially a child). Despite this; it's always quite difficult for them — as tears are frequently shed at our evening report.

- OB and it's many complications:

I deal with OB a lot in my book — for obvious reasons. It's our busiest area. So many babies are born in this setting, and thus the stage is set for the expected variations and complications. They are unexpected and endless. Personally I liked the challenge — really keeps you on your toes. Thanks to the OB texts I had! If they describe 100 variations and complications, I had 98 of them.

- Seizures (Convulsions):

I had to include seizures. They aren't rare in the USA; it's just that they are so common in Chimala. I'll say first that people everywhere are shocked by and frightened by seizures — usually don't know what to do. Add the factor that many people in Tanzania think seizures are satanic — that the patient has been bewitched. This results in their not wanting to touch a person in the midst of a seizure. The causes are myriad: meningitis, acute malaria, brain scarring from previous cerebral malaria, head injury, high fever, HIV/AIDS, encephalitis, liver and kidney diseases, electrolyte abnormalities, native medicine, overdoses, on and on.

I'm referring to what medically we call grand mal seizures. These are manifested by sudden, violent, asymmetrical jerking of all or part of the body. They are unresponsive and often make guttural-type sounds. There can be incontinence of urine or feces. The person can be bluish in color (cyanotic) because of ineffective breathing. They are violent and difficult to watch. The person can hurt themselves by thrashing about. I write more about seizures under, "All seizures eventually stop" in the section on "Truisms of Medicine".

- Where a Doctor is a Doctor is a Doctor?:

What do I mean by this? I became officially licensed in Tanzania in 1992 (by the way, this is a lifetime license without restrictions). By "no restrictions" I answered the question. If you are licensed as a Doctor, you can do anything — obstetrics, surgery, pediatrics, plastic surgery, and so forth. So as the mganga mkuu (chief doctor or doctor in charge) at Chimala, I had free reign to do whatever I thought best. Herein lies the difficulty. It is dependent upon the ability of the doctor, the facilities at the location, and the doctor's ego and good judgment as to what medical procedures are done. You can see this is a tremendous responsibility. I took it quite seriously.

I once wrote an abbreviated list in describing, "What is Third World Medicine."? This was done with a series of words:

- Crowds
- Filth
- Odors
- Delayed Care
- Poor Care
- No Care
- Huge pus cases
- Malnutrition
- Seizures galore
- Extreme suffering
- Much death
- Resolved, resolute, patient people
- Gratitude (from our patients)
- Tetanus cases
- Dying from snakebite
- Losing a leg from spear wound
- Too many burn cases
- Joy and sadness
- Reward and defeat (success and failure)
- Humbling for me
- Stretching our skills beyond our training
- Dying from diabetic ketoacidosis (no insulin available)
- Traction for six weeks (leg fracture)
- No oxygen oftentimes

- Frequent cancer of cervix and breast cancer (no Pap smears or mammography)
- High incidence of HIV/AIDS
- The list is endless!

"AXIOMS OF MEDICINE"
("Frankus Blackus" Style)

"Taking care of physical needs because of our compassion for the suffering may be the primary, over-riding reason for serving in healthcare missions; but beneath this reason should be our real ulterior motive — that being to follow the example of Jesus, the Great Physician."

Being an ER doc in America, there's a common thread that runs through all medicine — whether in a big city ER in America or a developing country's 'bush hospital'. Please take these "Axioms" (or "Truisms") with a grain of salt and a dash of doctor humor. No sacrilege or disrespect is intended, so take no offense.

Just remember that any of us who have been in the medical profession for any time have basically seen it all. We see many minor cases, but we are ready at a moment's notice to immediately drop what we're doing and see any emergency case. It's just that the lay public's definition of emergency would vary considerably from mine. By the way, I concocted this list on February 11, 1997 in Tanzania. The correlation with American medicine is amazing!

- <u>All bleeding eventually stops:</u>
  Now if you've jumped ahead of me, relax. I don't mean the patient has died. What this means is that if someone is in profound shock and the blood pressure has dropped precipitously, the bleeding will stop. Of course it's a dire situation and must be acted on immediately. This is the body's temporary response in trying to save itself. My point in this scenario is to get us (the medical profession) to relax, look for the cause, and perform the appropriate treatment promptly.

- <u>All seizures eventually stop:</u>
  Seizures (convulsions) are frightening in all cultures. Bleeding and seizures are the only two entities that my Tanzanian patients and fami-

lies reacted to as frantically as my USA cases. You should know that seizures are not a disease but are a <u>symptom</u> of some disease entity and its affect on the brain. We always look for the cause. Most seizures fortunately are relatively short lived and stop spontaneously. Of course we always act as quickly as possible when confronted with seizures. But it is a truism that "all seizures eventually stop." Probably 90% stop spontaneously within a few minutes. People worry about brain damage, but short-lived seizures do not cause this. Only quite prolonged seizures are worrisome in this regard — those lasting over 30 minutes. Medical therapy is not only to stop the active seizure but also to prevent others from recurring.

- <u>First of all, do no harm:</u>

This is the sine qua non of medicine. I cannot add to it. However, this statement does assume a different meaning in the context of being the only physician in a remote bush hospital. What do I mean? When I'm the only doctor within an hour's drive, there's no ambulance service, unsafe roads, combined with the uncertain presence or quality of doctors at another hospital, this axiom has to be adjusted. Therefore, I have to tackle cases I've never done before and take the risk. For me it boils down to this key point: If I think the chances are greater for my helping rather than harming the patient, I went for it. As you can readily see, this really puts the onus on me to be honest with myself — to not let pride blind my proper evaluation or overly rely on my medical ability. All this was not without significant trepidation. Experience proved this to be the best path to follow in a developing country's rural hospital. (I write about this several times, so you can see it was quite a significant factor for me.)

There just are not enough properly trained doctors in Tanzania, and this is especially true regarding specialists. Money is a huge factor. Some patients never get to see a doctor at the Government Hospital because they cannot pay. You read this correctly. The Government Referral Hospital in Mbeya had a "tiered" system. It clearly outlined who got what level of care, and the system was based exclusively on money.

I found that no matter what I attempted my patients had absolute confidence in me. They would choose me over one of their own country's doctors (just imagine this in the USA). I can't tell you how gratifying and humbling this was. Confidence begets confidence! It made me try even harder to do my very best at all times. It is one of my fondest memories of Tanzania, and an area that cannot be duplicated in my American practice.

- Time is the greatest healer:

Or better stated in our Missionary setting, *"God is the greatest healer"*. The inherent healing that God has instilled in our bodies is our best health ally. We totally relied on this fact and had it proved to us countless times. I had signs put up around the hospital that said: "Tunatibu magonjwa, lakina Mungu anayaponya". This is Swahili for, "We are treating the illnesses, but God is healing them." (My rendition of this truth is that the doctor's greatest ally is "tincture of time" — aka God's healing).

By the way, I stole the above statement from Dr. Henry Farrar. At Nigerian Christian Hospital he had signs that said, *"We dress the wound; God heals them"*.

- An important thing for a doctor to learn is 'when to do nothing':

This is kind of a corollary to the previous one. It means to stand back and think and wait; think and wait. If the patient is stable, this is often the best course of action.

- The more the complaints, the less the severity of the disease:

When someone has a severe, acute problem, it's amazing how few complaints there are. They are usually direct and specific — not nebulous and unrelated or non-specific. In other words, there is an inverse relationship between the number of complaints and the severity of the disease. But we must forever be cautious. Behind one of those seemingly innocuous complaints can be lurking a significant problem.

- Paitents can always "one up" the doctor on complaints:

     It's true of some patients that no matter how many complaints the doctor adequately deals with, they can always come up with another one — or two — or.... Another aspect of this is that in developing countries the patient may have never seen a doctor before — or at least very seldom. Consequently, they 'throw out' all the symptoms they've ever had — whether currently a problem or not. They may want medicine for something they've had in the past just in case the problem recurs.

- "You can lead a horse to water, but you can't make it drink:"

     Pardon my analogy here, but it does fit. A doctor can see a patient, properly diagnose, and give the proper medicine. But — but the doctor cannot be present and make sure the patient gets or takes the medicine or follows other instructions. Generally speaking, unless some procedure is done, the doctor only advises. The rest is up to the patient.

- You can't tell a patient they don't have pain (or the degree of pain):

     Pain is a symptom — not a disease. It is totally subjective. Different people with exactly the same problem or injury can act in polar opposite ways. For example, with a simple sprained ankle: One person will say, "Yes, it *hurts; but it's not that bad — just tape it up so I can get back in the game.*" Another person will lie there moaning continuously saying they cannot bear any weight on their ankle. The difference? Is it their perception of pain? Is the difference based on their personality? Is there indeed a difference in the pain? Is it a learned response? Remember, pain is subjective; so we can't answer these questions. There is no objective parameter to measure — unlike temperature or blood pressure.

- This is why I am so opposed to the American 1-10 pain scale!

     I can't have a section on pain without reiterating how amazingly tough the African is. (I know I write about this elsewhere. The simple repetition should point out the stark reality regarding the difference in pain response in cultures.). Africans tolerate pain to the nth degree without complaining. They put us Americans to shame. I think they grow up seeing people in pain and having pain themselves; therefore, it's expected and tolerated. The stoicism they uniformly display is part of their culture. Pain is expected; it's not feared and is not their enemy. They don't expect to be pain free. If I ordered pain medicine, the patients wouldn't ask for it, and the nurses usually wouldn't give it. WHY? Very pragmatically the nurses knew that certain entities were painful, so pain was to be expected and not necessary to be treated. Simple logic, huh! If I really wanted pain medicine to be administered, I had to write the order as a definite _"Give"_ (with a specific time listed). I couldn't just write to give it "PRN" (which means "as needed"). The nurses would interpret PRN as unnecessary. Even after surgery or in severe burn cases I would have to write the order as _"Give"_.

I also have to contrast the African response to pain with our too typical American response. Boy, I hardly know where to begin. Being an ER doc I see real pain, factitious pain, and over reaction to minor pain. The last two types listed are predominant, for we now have a tremendous problem in the USA with pain medicine abuse and addiction. What better place to go than the ER, where the patients don't know the doctor and vice versa. Remember; pain is subjective. The doctor has to make a judgment. Real pain? Level of pain? Drug seeker? You can never tell a patient they don't have pain or imply they don't have as much as they say — a sure way for a patient confrontation or complaint. As an analogy, try quantifying love; it's the same as trying to quantify pain.

When I returned from Africa and began working in an American ER, someone had come up with a PAIN SCALE. (??#!!@?!) I know you are all familiar with the scale. It's where patients can score their pain on a 1 to 10 scale (10 being the worst pain they could imagine and 1 being basically no pain). At best it's an artificial system, and most people have no way to compare. There's nothing objective about it — it's totally subjective.

Of course some people try and get "cutesy" with the Pain Scale and say, "Oh, it's an 11 — or _20_" — or whatever. When all this is factored in, we have to make a judgment. Some patients seem to think that a higher score will get them more pain medicine. Others are outright making a play for unnecessary pain medicine. This has become one of the biggest sources of consternation for an ER doc — trying to 'appease' patients who supposedly have some type chronic pain and are using the ER for their pain prescription or are "out right" drug seekers. (Wow, do we hear some great stories!). It's one of our biggest sources of conflict in the ER. Isn't this a shame when I should be concerned about that serious cardiac arrhythmia in room #10 or whether I should do a spinal tap on the 2 year old in room #16. I shouldn't have to worry about a possible complaint from a patient with chronic back pain for whom I refused to prescribe narcotics. SOMETHING IS WRONG WITH THIS PICTURE!

I'm sorry; I got carried away. But seriously; Americans, unlike the Africans, view pain as the enemy — something to be alleviated <u>now</u>. Our culture and even our medical profession has helped foster this view. We are now reaping the results with our huge drug abuse and narcotic addiction problem.

- <u>La belle indifference'</u>:
The dictionary definition for this French phrase is, "Inappropriate lack of concern for the implications of one's disability." Practically speaking it means that a patient can look comfortable and unconcerned, yet at the same time they are giving a litany of severe symptoms or speaking of severe pain. The face and posturing of the patient does not match what they are saying. What does this mean to you? Frankly, it's the same for us physicians. You tend not to believe what is being said. But as a physician, you have to maintain objectivity and not jump to conclusions. This behavior transcends culture and can be used as a helpful diagnostic aid, whether in Tanzania or in Indianapolis.

- <u>Can't judge the severity of the wound by the amount of blood visible</u>:
A patient can present with blood running down their face and a blood-soaked towel wrapped around their head. Upon removing the

towel and cleaning the wound, sometimes you find no more than a small scalp puncture wound. Conversely, a patient can present pale, clammy, and in shock and have nothing more than a small stab wound of the abdomen. Upon surgical exploration they can have a belly full of blood from a perforated artery. Bottom line: Clean and explore the wound and examine the whole patient.

- <u>Can't judge the severity of the disease or injury by the emotional response of the patient or their accompanying loved ones:</u>

   Hysteria can reign in any culture. It can take an experienced medical person to decipher what is an injury or disease and what is the psychological overlay — emotional response.

- <u>Can't judge severity of disease by the number of doctors the patient has seen:</u>

   The patient can turn out to be quite persistent — a hypochondriac or a chronic complainer who keeps hopping from doctor to doctor, always looking for "The Answer" to their problems. Always try to get previous medical records (next to impossible in Africa)

- <u>The Medical History:</u>

   The Medical History represents the answers obtained from verbal questioning of the patient or others who have information regarding the illness or injury. When I was in Medical School at Vanderbilt taking Physical Diagnosis, I was taught that the most important part of the patient encounter was the medical history. If you just asked the right questions and were astute enough, you could diagnose almost 80% of cases. I would reverse that number in Africa — saying that perhaps 20% of cases could be diagnosed on the basis of the medical history alone. Why is this? I think it's a combination of reasons. The patient thinks that the more symptoms they have, the more the doctor will take note. They often give all the symptoms they've ever had. They don't know as much about their bodies or diseases; therefore, they don't know what is important. It's can become what we call a "positive review of systems" (no negative answers). Because the medical history becomes less important in our setting, it consequently renders the physical exam ever more important. Examine, examine; observe and examine some more!

- "FSP":

What do you call it when the doctor has no idea what the problem is or what to do? Remember that I had a very limited laboratory and other means of testing. But you have to do something. Here's where FSP comes in. You make your <u>best educated guess</u> as to what is wrong and treat accordingly. So FSP stands for, *"Flying by the Seat of your Pants"*. No, it's not a blind stab in the dark. After contemplation and using your experience and any resources available, you make your decision — your best educated guess -(judgment sounds better).

- "Veterinary Medicine" ("VM"):

There was a small tribe in the mountains behind our mission that lived in seclusion and was totally independent. They were quite primitive. They dressed differently, spoke differently, and had quite different tribal markings. The women wore leather outfits, complete with skirts. They had peculiar circular tribal markings around their eyes. We thought this gave them an 'owl-like' look. What was most striking was that they spoke their own language and didn't speak the national language (Swahili). We had hospital staff that spoke a number of tribal languages, but no one spoke theirs. So, here I am trying to be their doctor and can speak no verbal language with them. Some gestures are 'universal' and do help, but basically I'm left with my physical exam, observation, and what testing we have.

Lou Ann doesn't like for me to say what I'm about to say. I want to quickly add that in no way is this considered a "put down" or trying to poke fun. It just came to me one day, and it does fit. Without further ado, what do you call it when you can't speak to your 'patients' or their families? How about "Veterinary Medicine"? Think about it. If you take your sick dog for care, the vet can't talk to your canine. Rover is not able to give a history, but the owner usually does contribute. I had no one to contribute to the patient's history from the tribe I mentioned. Anyway, it seemed to me to be a valid analogy to "VM".

- Success Breeds Success:

Translated this means, *"You get busier and busier."* We (Janice, Tanzanian medical staff, and I) provided timely, good quality medical care to the people of Chimala. We cared, and they knew it. Through our "Work Fund" Lou Ann and I were able to substantially add to the supplies necessary to run a hospital. We were constantly improving our patient care services. Over time this information spreads by word of mouth. The result is that we had more and more patients as time passed. It was not unusual for people to come by bus from more than an hour away in order to get our opinion or treatment. We even had women come this far who needed Caesarean sections. Over our five years at Chimala our C-section rate doubled. This was from having more total patients — not from an increased population, other facilities closing, or doing C-sections for convenience sake. We only performed them when either the mother or baby or both were in jeopardy.

Getting busier is good and it's bad. What do I mean? It's good because we provided the care to more people, and they subsequently had a healthier and longer life. It's bad from the standpoint that we had to do all the work with no additional help. I know this sounds self-serving. You might be thinking, *"Isn't that what you went there for"*. Well yes, but we needed more help. The mental and physical fatigue really wears on you. Yours truly can attest to this. I've seen very good doctors "chewed up and spit out" by working so hard for so long in very busy missionary hospitals. Some of these doctors were so psychologically damaged that they never returned to missionary medical work. The lesson? Go with a medical team; set limits; take enough time off. Easier said than done.

A DAY IN THE LIFE OF........

"As another day's work begins, I am aware that just anything can happen! It may be a day in which everything runs like clockwork (most unlikely), or it may be a day packed with emergencies, admissions, crying babies, questions, countless visitors, constant interruptions, and never ending work. But I know, Lord, that whatever the situation I am to represent You. Be with me in a special way today, that I may not fail You!"

–John Fuller
(This quote was taped on the wall by my desk. It inspired me each and every day.)

Our 88 bed bush hospital averaged 'over capacity' each year. What does this mean? It means that we averaged over 88 patients per day for each of the 365 days of the year. We were especially busy during certain months — up to the range of 120-130 patients during malaria season (March through June). You're probably asking, "Where did you put the patients?" We often put two patients per bed. These would be the sickest ones and the ones with IV's. The remainder of the patients became "floor cases." Don't worry; we did have some mattresses to put on the floor — placed either between the beds or in the corridors. If we ran out of mattresses, the patients slept on a mat.

I'll add here that over the course of our five years at Chimala our patient volume steadily increased. Why was this? No; it wasn't population growth or some other nearby medical facility closing. I'd like to think it was because of our good, compassionate care. (I give much of the credit to Lou Ann and to Janice. "Dr. Janice" and her running of the Pediatric Ward). The type of care we tried to administer is so appreciated and knowledge of such a team spread quickly by 'word of mouth'. It's true that the presence of American medical personnel virtually always will bring about an increase in patient volume. I knew it wasn't because of me personally, but it is still quite humbling to be so respected. Jokingly I said, *"Build it and they will come."*

I typically made rounds on male ward, female ward, and OB. When we had "floor cases", you'd find me stepping over and around these patients. Of course when I stopped to examine them, I'd have to get down on my knees. It's always important to get close to your patient — to touch them and to do some examination. I was always available to help Janice on Pediatrics at any time. Rounds often went from 8:15 till lunch around noonish and then beyond. It was the norm to be interrupted during rounds by emergencies, procedures, new admissions, and of course OB.

I'll take you on some rounds now. This particular day was just as it was recorded in my log book:

February 2, 1997 [Female Ward]

1. 24 year old who is quite confused — cause unknown — being worked up for HIV — (came back positive)
2. 26 year old two days post-op for a pelvic abscess; fever; suspected venereal disease
3. 17 year old very septic (infected) — six days post-op following abdominal exploratory surgery for a large pus-filled abscess along the descending colon. Cause uncertain.
4. 19 year old following a D&C (dilatation and curettage) for an incomplete spontaneous abortion (miscarriage)
5. 16 year old with a seizure disorder and severe burns to the feet — (I've written more completely about Furahini elsewhere)
6. 23 year old new diagnosis of HIV/AIDS — very thin, weak, with fever
7. 35 year old malaria case
8. 32 year old quite ill with pneumonia — suspected HIV/AIDS
9. 40 year old with a severe ankle fracture
10. 27 year old D&C
11. 23 year old new mother (one month old baby) with a tender pelvic mass — (post delivery infection)
12. 34 year old with malaria and abdominal pain
13. 21 year old new HIV/AIDS case in coma (unresponsive)

14. 31 year old malaria case
15. 22 year old new HIV/AIDS case — very thin, weak
16. 32 year old with large injection abscess in the buttocks (this is secondary to an intramuscular injection)
17. 26 year old D&C
18. 38 year old — very weak; pneumonia (not HIV/AIDS)
19. New patient: 41 year old with ascites (this is fluid retained within the abdominal cavity; usually from severe liver disease, such as cirrhosis from hepatitis, alcohol, etc.)
20. Elderly woman (guessed to be 60ish) — didn't know her age. Severe back pain and scoliosis (curvature of spine), suspected tuberculosis
21. 26 year old with torn knee ligament with effusion (fluid within the joint)
22. 15 year old with minor reaction to snake bite (pain, swelling)
23. 23 year old with new HIV/AIDS — very thin, weak, diarrhea
24. 19 year old D&C
25. 35 year old "beaten case". Multiple severe bruises from husband abuse. (Such abuse is almost "expected" here and the woman basically has no recourse. The local police will do nothing. On one occasion I had five ladies in the hospital simultaneously with serious injuries from abuse: broken arm; broken ribs; broken jaw; broken leg; broken nose and severe bruising. Even on that occasion I could get no help from the police.)
26. Another older lady (age ?) — pneumonia
27. 45 year old obese lady with severe neck pain — cause unknown. (Yes, we occasionally would see obese people. This usually meant they had more education and more money. Consequently, they had more and better food and medical care.)
28. 14 year old with intra-abdominal bleeding from a spleen injury. (Ultimately she recovered well with no surgery).

This was basically an average day on the ward. What is easily noticeable to me, however, is the lack of malaria cases. February is still in the dry season before the rains start and usher in the throes of malaria. I might ask you what is noticeable to you about the list? One thing you should notice is the age of the patients. Look how young they are! The average life span when we went to Tanzania was about 50, so you just didn't see many older people. And yes, they thought anyone over 50 was old. (I was 50 when I moved to Tanzania, and they couldn't believe I was that old — combination of my blessed genetics, my conservative and easy life style, and good medical care). Families oftentimes wouldn't bring their 'older' family members for health care. You're probably asking why? This would be anathema in the USA — not to mention being called "elder abuse" and being criminally liable. The answer is one of priority and practicality. The families had very little money, so they would spend it on the younger people. And being brutally practical, what happens to older people? They die. Remember; the average life expectancy was only about 50. "Why spend money on an older person when they were going to die soon anyway?" Sounds awful, doesn't it!? Of course I don't believe this and never fostered this type thinking. But you can understand their logic. This does present somewhat of a paradox, for Tanzanians love and respect their parents and their elders. They lovingly take care of them at home as best they can for as long as they can. Yet they may not seek medical care.

(Tragically the average life span decreased below 50 because of the ravages of HIV/AIDS)

I'm sure you noticed the variety of cases and how many had various surgeries. It's true that yours truly performed the surgeries; and no, many of these operations I had never seen, much less done. I tell more about this in the chapter, "Surgery By a Non-surgeon." By adhering to good basic surgical rules and techniques, and knowing what "not to do", most patients did well.

There were several HIV/AIDS cases on this particular day. This would be a stark difference from your average American hospital female ward. And actually the number of cases on this particular day was a lot less than we usually had. As I've said in the chapter on HIV/AIDS, we tried to minimize the hospitalizations and the length of stay. Even though a missionary hospital, the families were still charged a fee. Many families spent all they had on their loved ones with HIV/AIDS. Medical insurance was an unknown entity at this time.

You noticed quite a few patients who had D&C's. This is the procedure needed for patients who have spontaneous abortions (miscarriages) and continue to have heavy bleeding. These are called incomplete abortions because all the products of conception are not expelled from the uterus. Why so many incomplete abortions? The answer is simple. It's because they have so many babies, and spontaneous abortions occur in about 10% of pregnancies. Being a male dominant culture, one of the women's "jobs" is to provide offspring — especially sons.

While dealing with this subject, you need to know that performing abortions was illegal when we were in Tanzania. Also it was still a taboo and an insult for an unmarried woman to become pregnant — a shame for their families. Many of these young pregnant women resorted to drastic measures in order to terminate their pregnancies surreptitiously. They didn't want especially their fathers to know. Some took abortigenic local potions that would cause them to abort. Others would go to people who performed criminal abortions in order to terminate the pregnancy. I saw women who died from these attempts — either from bleeding, infection, or toxicity to the drugs used. I saw some young unmarried women who attempted suicide (some succeeded) because of the shame their pregnancies caused for their families.

One particular day I had two life threatening emergencies caused by attempts at a criminal abortion. The first lady was in shock (very low blood pressure) from excessive bleeding caused by tears from the criminal procedure. I had to give her transfusions and take her to surgery in order to repair the damage. The second lady was in shock, had fever, and had what we call an "acute abdomen" (when there is severe pain and exquisite tenderness all throughout the abdomen to palpation — examination with your hand). This is also called peritonitis. I took her to surgery and found that she had a perforated uterus from the criminal abortion. This had led to her severe infection and shock. In surgery I repaired the damage to the uterus and put her on high doses of IV antibiotics. Thankfully she recovered from this near fatal situation. Her sexual activity outside marriage almost cost her life — not to mention the shame and expense to her family.

"DOCTOR, IT'S ALL HANGING OUT"

"Recognizing the problem is a problem half solved."

Lest I gross you out; I want to register a disclaimer. Those of you who are offended by discussion of blood and body parts or the sometimes sacrilegious 'doctor speak' ['medicalese'], please pass on this section. I'm kind of joking, but I did want to warn you. I hope you realize that absolutely no disrespect is meant when I occasionally speak of gross or sad things in 'doctor speak.'

As I've written elsewhere, obstetrics was the area that always kept us on our toes. Never; I repeat; never do you have "control" of Obstetrics. It is entirely random and fraught with an exhausting variety of complications. The only thing predictable about OB is its unpredictability. This is increased in part because of living in a remote African village where the average number of pregnancies is eight to ten. Add in the lack of prenatal care, frequent local self-proclaimed "mid-wives", and you have the formula for OB complications.

This chapter title was not made up. These are the exact words used by a nurse who came to my house one night. (Usually they would just say, "shida OB" — this means "problem in OB"). Naturally I was quite used to the unusual — always expecting the unexpected. So I hurried down to the hospital's labor room. What I found was quite apparent by one look. The lady had a hand, a foot, and the cord hanging out of her vagina. Even if you are totally unfamiliar with obstetrics, you must know this is most unusual and fraught with trouble. It is a most unusual presentation (we use the term "presentation" to describe what body part is presenting at the introitus — the opening of the vagina). You can imagine the contortion the baby would be in by presenting this way. It would usually cause fetal demise, as it did in this particular case (no fetal heart tones were heard). The baby often loses its oxygen supply because the cord, which supplies the oxygen from mother's blood, is kinked or compressed. I had to perform a Caesarean section in order to remove the dead baby and prevent further damage to the mother.

Of course the usual and normal way for a baby to present is cephalic (head first). A breech is a baby that presents feet or buttocks first. These babies can usually be delivered vaginally. The case above was unusual because it had three different parts presenting (hand, foot, and cord). Usually there's just one part protruding, such as a hand, a foot, the buttocks, the cord, an elbow, a shoulder — use your imagination. If it can happen, it will in OB. Many such presentations cannot be delivered vaginally without severe damage to the baby and the mother. Therefore, a Caesarean section becomes necessary as an emergency — to save the baby.

I must say that our midwives did an outstanding job with what they had available. Remember that they had no fetal monitoring. When they detected a problem with labor, fetal presentation, or the fetal heart rate, I would be called to evaluate the situation. I listened for the baby's heart beat with my stethoscope — sometimes for many minutes. This is much easier with a Doppler, which I was able to obtain later (a hand-held electronic device that is moved around on the mother's abdomen until you hear the heart beat). Usually by this assessment I could tell if the baby was in 'distress' (this is the term that's used when the baby is in trouble). The most common indication of distress is when the baby's heart rate is too slow (or occasionally too fast). If this sign of distress occurred, we usually would operate within an hour.

(More about Caesarian sections in another chapter.)

JESUS AND HEALING

Luke 9:2 — *"He sent His disciples out to preach the kingdom of God and to heal the sick."*

(I considered this verse to be my mandate — my 'marching orders'.)

Being a Christian means I'm a follower of Jesus Christ. Jesus was many things, and among them he was a healer. We like to say that Jesus was God's only Son and the first medical missionary. The New Testament tells specifically of some thirty-five miracles. Of these, twenty-three involved healing, three were raised from the dead, and nine showed his power over nature. We know there were many more, for the Bible says, "...... *he healed all who came*".

Why did Jesus heal people? He knew that just like today, peoples' health was their number one concern. He had <u>compassion</u> on the human condition — suffering. I think this was his primary reason. Of course miracles also showed his power, but this seemed secondary. They also drew attention to him, but this also was probably not his primary motive. Basically he healed people because he cared. He had no pre-requisites for healing. He healed all comers. He required nothing — not even that they would stay and listen to him speak or become a follower.

Being a Christ follower and a physician, I always wanted to use my medical training and my Christianity together. How to do this? My answer came by way of becoming a medical missionary. This allowed me to serve medically where the need was so great; to not worry about financial, legal, or administrative matters; but to just do the most I could to help peoples' health — both physical and spiritual. I was always able to teach, pray, and represent Christianity in a myriad of ways on the missionary field.

"People are much more willing to hear what you have to say if you first show them that you care."

On the Scene with "Dr. Jesus"

What was it like? Word would quickly spread that this man (named Jesus) was reported to be able to heal people. He was probably the only 'show' in town — no malls, movie theaters, or sports arenas. So of course people would 'check it out'. Curiosity would have been the biggest incentive to see this man. And once they saw that people were indeed healed, flocks of sick would come. And come they did. We are told that they followed him, came to him at night — inundating him. Generally he healed each one face to face — touching them. I'm sure at some point he needed "crowd control" and turned over the sick to his disciples, as he would begin to speak and tell people about his Father God.

When I worked in Tanzania, I couldn't help but think of my situation as being similar in some ways to that of Jesus. Please don't misunderstand. I certainly have no thoughts of grandeur or a messianic complex. These are just simplistic comparisons. Like Jesus we were always inundated by the sick and disabled. There seemed to be an endless stream of people and their needs. We could never take care of all the needs. And remember that our brand of medicine at Chimala was quite rudimentary. Sometimes in the midst of the day with the hospital full, four new admissions, two C-sections pending, a spinal tap to do, and two burn patients to debride, I wondered how I could possibly do it all. My mind would wander to what it was like for Jesus with the throngs all around him. Somehow this thought and a prayer in my heart would give me comfort and the ability to keep going.

Most people in Chimala lived not much differently than the people of Jesus' day. Most lived without running water or electricity, in mud huts with thatched roofs. They walked everywhere they went. The quality of medical care outside our hospital was given by 'native medicine doctors' using various roots and herbs and sacrifices. The people knew little more about their bodies and disease than the people of Jesus' time.

We also saw 'all comers'; we refused no one. There were no requirements for being seen. Yes, we charged a fee; but those who had no money were all treated the same.

Humorously, I've had various thoughts as to Jesus and his healing. So bear with me.

- He took on all comers — he was the "ultimate specialist"
- No requirement of money, insurance, etc. — FREE!
- He needed no history or physical exam
- 100% cure rate — instantaneously!
- No pain
- 100% satisfaction rate — no complaints
- No tests needed — lab, X-ray, etc.
- No medicine needed
- No office staff
- No casts, splints, or physical therapy
- No complications
- No follow-up requirement — total healing

Wow, how we physicians could fantasize about this! For the most part we are not told what happened to the people Jesus healed. How many followed him? How many told others? Of course the ones healed or raised from the dead would have gotten sick again and died.

Could Jesus have healed more? Yes. But this wasn't the point. The point was to present himself and his Father God, so that people would follow them. He could have done generic healing or healing en masse, but he used a personalized approach. I really like this, don't you? I think it's important, and I try to individualize my practice as much as possible.

I'll conclude this section with some words I wrote in the past:

"We as medical missionaries are God's lowly servants, tools or instruments, to help his inherent healing in ways that he has allowed mankind to

discover. We are his allies in compassionately trying to heal or relieve suffering on the physical side (mankind's greatest concern) while addressing the spiritual side (mankind's greatest need).

It gives me great comfort and strength to know that Jesus knows exactly what we combat and go through."

TOO LITTLE — TOO MUCH

"Be content with what you have — but not with what you are."

Okay; you be the judge. Does an American standard ER exam room have too much "stuff" or do our Chimala rooms have too little. The answer is rather obvious; but it begs the question — do our American rooms have entirely too much? First I'll do the easy part. That's to tell you what the standard room or entire ward had available at Chimala Mission Hospital.

- Clinic rooms usually had a desk, two chairs, and perhaps a flat long wooden table (this sufficed as an exam table). There might have been a rolling, portable screen for privacy. You'd have to hunt rather long and hard to even find a trash can, much less other amenities.

- Most of the clinic rooms had an overhead ceiling light that would work if the electricity was functional.

- The wards were long rectangular rooms with about twenty beds — ten lined up on one side and ten on the other, with a walkway between the beds. There were overhead fluorescent lights, with some "sky lights" in the ceiling as an added daytime light source. Each bed, which looked like an army barracks bed, had a very thin mattress. Yes, we did have sheets and blankets. Remember that most of our patients slept on a woven mat on the floor in their huts. At one point we actually used old Army cots when we needed more beds. Later we did get some rather ancient but actual hospital-type beds. Some of the cranks for raising or lowering the head or feet actually worked! There was a small bedside table or small cabinet where the patient could put food or personal items. Initially there was not even one blood pressure cuff (sphygmomanometer) for each ward. Later we got some mercury column sphygmomanometers — the type that rolls around on wheels but haven't been used in American hospitals in thirty-five years.

- Yes, that's it! What would you think is missing? (And your being on a ward with 19 other patients doesn't count.)

Now for the exhausting list of what is in every standard room of your local Emergency Department:

- One Stryker. This "bed" has every adjustment imaginable and then some — controlled electrically by buttons. And believe it or not, it's much more comfortable than our Chimala beds. There's even a pillow for each Stryker.
- Overhead lighting, complete with rheostat. There's also separate subdued lighting just for the head end of the bed.
- Adjustable overhead surgical lighting
- A curtain suspended from the ceiling which slides around the bed
- A ceiling mounted metal track with suspended IV hangers
- Two chairs
- One soiled linen hamper
- Three waste cans
- Hangers for clothes mounted on the wall
- Writing board on the wall
- Sink with hot and cold water — of course a soap dispenser and paper towel dispenser
- Can't forget the ubiquitous wall mounted flat screen TV complete with a remote controller
- Nurse call button
- Two wall mounted glove dispensers — in small, medium, and large sizes
- Two wall mounted "sharps" disposal containers
- Wall mounted otoscope/ophthalmoscope unit (for examining ears and eyes)
- Wall mounted blood pressure (BP) unit

- Monitor with measurements for pulse, BP, respiratory rate, oxygen saturation, and EKG (electrocardiogram for heart rate and rhythm)
- Wall oxygen dispenser
- Wall suction
- Kleenex tissues
- Several large cabinets stuffed full of various supplies, so that neither nurse nor doctor have to 'run around' to find needed items
- WHEW! I'm sure I've left off a number of things?

What do you think? Too much or too little? How about a bit of both.

"PATIENCE AND EFFICIENCY?"

"A great journey is begun with the first step."

(Or in relation to this chapter; "If the Egyptians could build the pyramids, then ......")

One of the many qualities I don't possess is that of patience. (Just ask Lou Ann). Actually a good spin off resulting from being an inherently impatient person is that it leads to efficiency. (How do you like that for my defense?). I was really up against it in Chimala. I was told by one Tanzanian that they didn't have a Swahili word for efficiency. That pretty well sums it up! This was a real challenge for me — kind of like mixing oil and water. I fought this (I think that's the right word to use) for my entire five years. I did find out that I just couldn't impose my efficiency on the Tanzanians. Sure I tried and did have a few minor improvements here and there. But when push came to shove, their basic ways always won out. I finally relented and just tried to be as efficient as I could in the culture.

Efficiency doesn't always mean speed of action. You can do something quickly but poorly. Efficiency is thinking something through, seeing the best course of action, and then going about it quickly and directly with focus.

Being the most efficient also means having others help. It can be an assistant at your side, a runner ("gopher" — go for this; go for that) to get things for you, and others who know their role.

I should interject that Lou Ann became my "chief gopher". This is not a derogatory term by the way; it's a term of endearment. She knew what we had, where it was, and how to get to it. When she was on the scene, things went much more smoothly and efficiently.

The operating room should be a good example of efficiency at work — the surgeon, a knowledgeable assistant (one who scrubs in with the surgeon), scrub nurse (who passes instruments), an anesthetist, at least one 'circulator' (someone to keep the needed supplies quickly available).

I might add that a poor surgical assistant is probably worse than no one at all. They are supposed to be thinking one step ahead of the surgeon — when to cut, when to use suction, when and what kind of suture is needed, when to retract, and many other things. If you have to constantly tell the assistant what to do or wait on them, it's almost better not to have the assistant. They become a liability and not an asset. I'll add here that in Chimala where many patients were HIV positive, we had the added risk of "needle sticks" — which meant immediate exposure to the virus. A poor assistant might not always handle the needles and sharp instruments properly, thus increasing the risk. There were some assistants with whom I wouldn't scrub because of this danger.

It just was not possible to have 100% efficiency in our setting. I accepted this but constantly tried for the best we could do. We were limited by not enough personnel, some poorly trained personnel, limited supplies (and knowledge of what we had and where it was), missing or inadequate equipment, on again off again electricity, and the list goes on. Let me go through an example of what I did on just one case as I recorded in my journal (the antithesis of efficiency):

1) A teenaged boy arrived on this Saturday afternoon at 2:30, having sustained a broken femur. I went to the hospital, saw his X-ray, and proceeded to set up his traction.

2) Went to Minor Theatre II to get supplies. I had my key, but the door was already open. Unlocked the cabinet but none of my needed supplies were where they should have been. Locked the door.

3) Unlocked the pharmacy to get some syringes and needles.

4) Unlocked Minor Theatre I to get xylocaine, betadine, and antibiotic ointment.

5) Locked Minor I but had to return to get a surgical blade I'd forgotten.

6) Went to Minor II again to look for rope and a weight bag — for traction

7) Unlocked my office to get sterile gloves and some tape
8) Unlocked surgery to get the sterile traction kit. I looked through three cabinets but found it.

(Janice had found some rope)

9) Looked on male and female ward for the device to elevate his leg and for the weight bag — (This was a large plastic bag that held water and had a marked scale showing what volume of water and its weight.). The weight in a bag used for traction was to keep the bone in position and was determined by a percentage of the patient's weight.
10) The one door I didn't have a key for on male ward turned out to have the needed supplies. I found the key at the nurses' station.
11) I needed the patient to move to another bed that would fit the traction device. Without waiting for my help, a male nursing student then proceeded to pick up the boy and whisked him to the new bed. Ouch! The pain! There seemed to be no thought about moving him carefully, so as not to move his fractured femur (upper leg) and invoke severe pain.
12) Faulty equipment: After cleaning the area, the skin and subcutaneous tissue is anesthetized with xylocaine. Then a metal pin is actually placed transversally through the bone (tibia) just below the knee. I know this sounds rather gross, but it is effective and was done this way in the USA until the '60's. A mechanical drill is used in placing the pin through the bone. My drill wouldn't tighten down on the pin, so it kept slipping instead of penetrating the bone (the tightening key used on the drill was long gone].
13) Would you believe Janice went to my house to get a hammer — that's right; a hammer. The young man stoically lay there as I used my hammer to finish getting the pin through his tibia. Yes, he was awake during all this. Remember, I always talk about the Tanzanian's remarkable acceptance and tolerance of pain.
14) I finished with his dressing, attached the various and sundry orthopedic paraphernalia, positioned his leg, put the rope

over the pulley to the weighted water bag, elevated the end of his bed, and <u>FINISHED.</u> (Before we found these neat water bags for weight, I used cloth bags filled with sand, measured to the needed weight.)

He tolerated the procedure quite well and the traction was just as I wanted it — positioning the fractured bone ends properly. Unfortunately, I didn't record the amount of time this took, but it was probably in the range of an hour and a half. The actual procedure probably only took 10-15 minutes. The extra time involved finding all the necessary supplies — ones that work. In all fairness I should remind you that this was on a Saturday afternoon. The Hospital's regular fully staffed hours were basically from 8AM to 5PM Monday through Friday and Saturday mornings. At other hours we had limited staff and many locked areas. The whole process would have gone more quickly and "efficiently" during fully staffed hours. But I hasten to add that what I've written above is definitely not an unusual occurrence. Emergencies have an uncanny way of occurring at odd times — especially nights and weekends. (Being an emergency physician in the USA I can fully attest to this.).

Now back to the subject of patience. After relating the above situation, "My case rests" regarding efficiency. I saw the case through to its successful conclusion — and didn't 'blow my cool'. I remained patient. I can't say I always managed as well. How would you do in these situations? Would you remain patient? I may have difficulty with patience, but I also have the God-given trait of perseverance. It's equally as important to stay on task until the task is successfully completed.

I mentioned being personally as efficient as possible. Elsewhere I told of how I did bedside spinal taps and having all the needed supplies in my "magic green bag".

Tanzanians set the standard for patience! No doubt about it. (Efficiency: oh well, you can't have everything). One hallmark of a developing country is WAITING. They seem to wait for everything: at the clinic, for a bus ride, at the post office and all offices, at work and school, and everywhere. Another area where we Americans differ drastically from Tanzanians is that of the patience to wait. To wait is anathema for most Americans! It brings out the worst behavior in many and contributes to the "Ugly American" image.

I can't leave this topic without my best example of Tanzanian inefficiency. Now this wouldn't be considered inefficient if it's the best you can do — and it was. But compared to what you would expect in the USA; this situation is first of all quite amazing and after that, most primitive.

On a trip to Dar we had just begun our descent of the mountain range outside Iringa. These were major mountains with the two-lane road winding precariously back and forth while overlooking precipitous drops into the chasm below — no guard rails of course. On almost every trip we would see evidence far below of yet another vehicle or container that had succumbed to the conditions. As we slowly and carefully were navigating another hairpin curve, we saw a lot of smoke up ahead. Naturally we thought that a vehicle had wrecked and was ablaze. As we approached, the amount of smoke made it difficult to tell what was burning. When we finally could make out what it was, we were flabbergasted. Yes, this is true. A huge boulder the size of a truck was obstructing half the roadway and was on fire. Okay; now what is this all about? It seems that the huge boulder had fallen onto the roadway from the cliffs above. I don't know how long it had been there. As I ascertained, here's what was happening. Without the necessary heavy equipment available, the local people were trying to remove the boulder from the narrow roadway as best they could. They doused it with kerosene and lit it. The subsequent heat supposedly would make the boulder more brittle. Then several men would keep attacking it with their sledgehammers with the expectation of slowly breaking up the monstrous hunk. As we passed by in our vehicle, they were pounding away. ——- On our return trip there was no evidence of the boulder — only a somewhat blackened spot on the roadway. Patience and persistence, but not efficiency.

THE "MYSTERY" OF THE BROKEN FEMURS

*"The man who tries to do something and fails is a lot better off than
the man who tries to do nothing and succeeds."*

Fairly often we had infants come to the hospital with the typical findings of a broken femur (upper leg bone). They would be in obvious
severe pain and have the findings of a very tender, swollen thigh. In
these cases an X-ray wasn't even necessary to make the diagnosis, but of
course we always obtained one. Now I'm talking about infants who are
not yet able to walk or climb. So how did they break their femurs?
Remember that the femur is the largest and strongest bone in the body.
It would take quite a force to break the femur. In the cases we had we
were never able to obtain a history of trauma. In the USA such unexplained cases are always child abuse until proven otherwise. Usually
broken femurs are the result of very severe trauma such as crush injuries,
car or motorcycle accidents, falls from a height, child abuse, etc. Child
abuse is essentially unheard of in Tanzania. So we had a mystery on our
hands. Our 'inside medical humor' called the Tanzanian femur their
weakest bone. So how did this happen — what was the mechanism of
injury?

I figured it out. The babies are always carried on their Mother's
back in a wrapper. But frequently the babies' little sisters carried their
younger siblings. Some of these girls were only five or six. You can
imagine a girl perhaps of forty to fifty pounds carrying a baby of perhaps
twenty pounds. They can become top heavy and overbalanced with the
baby on their back. If the baby begins to fall backwards, the small girl
would not be strong enough to adjust and rectify the situation. The baby
would continue falling backwards while their legs are held down by the
wrapper. As the baby fell, their entire weight and the resultant force
would be exerted at a point near the mid portion of their femur. This
then would result in a break. It's just like you had a stick with one end

in each hand that was then bent and bent until "snap" — the same mechanism. Mystery solved.

So what did we do with these infants with fractured femurs. We used what is called "gallows traction". As the baby lay on its back, I put a soft dressing around both ankles, attached these dressings to a suspending cord, tied the cord over the bed so that the baby's hips were suspended barely off the bed. Sounds most awkward and uncomfortable, doesn't it? Actually it wasn't. The babies tolerated this 'device' remarkably well. What it did was use the babies' own weight as traction on the fracture, so that the bone would be in proper position to heal. Believe it or not, the babies would stay like this for about four weeks. Healing is quite fast in babies. Remember that they don't walk yet, so consequently we didn't have to worry about weight bearing when their traction was removed. We almost always had very good results. You wouldn't believe the contortions the babies went through while in the traction. They did everything, almost including back flips. It obviously was not painful to them.

"THE MIGHTY HUNTER"

"Almost anything you do will be insignificant, but it is important that you do it."

— M. Ghandi

This title is with "tongue in cheek", for I am anything but a hunter. I think I shot some birds with my BB gun as a young boy. Perhaps a squirrel or two as a teenager. And nothing since. Don't get me wrong; I have no objection to hunting or killing animals. It's just that my interests took me in other directions.

This now takes me to Tanzania. We lived pretty much in bush country, and some big game animals still lived in our area. It was illegal to hunt in Game Parks but was legal (with proper licenses) in other areas — including ours. It was the habit of some of our ex-patriot missionaries to hunt from time to time. We indeed loved the meat they would bring back — impala, water buck, topi, etc. The beef we were able to buy was really very poor quality, so we had pretty much given up on beef. The wild game filled that void. I must say that this meat was less 'gamey' than that of Indiana deer, which my son hunted.

It seemed that the hunters on our compound always hunted on the weekends I was on-call. I really wasn't looking for a chance to go, but finally an opportunity came. And how! The owners of a nearby hunting safari business offered us two days of free hunting. They had a last minute cancellation and wanted to show their appreciation for the medical care they received from us. This was quite a gift, for they ordinarily charged $800 per day plus the 'tags' to kill the various animals. Since I had a resident permit in Tanzania, I qualified for the local rates. Instead of $400 for a Cape buffalo tag, I paid $60 (I bought two). Instead of $200 for impala and wart hog tags, I paid $40 for each.

So off we 'mighty hunters' went. Lou Ann shared the adventure. All we had to do was show up. The outfitters took care of everything else — and I mean everything. They drove us, set up camp, cooked delicious meals, washed our clothes, and even had a set up for a hot shower — a 55 gallon drum had been put on a platform with a raging fire underneath. A pipe from the drum led to an enclosed 'shower stall', complete with shower head. Very nice! There was even a wooden floor in our tents. All this before we started hunting early the next morning. It all reminded me of some old movies I'd seen of a hunting safari in Africa — perhaps "The Snows of Kilimanjaro."

We took off the next morning in our Land Rover-type hunting vehicles with the open back for standing and shooting. You've seen them in movies. The trackers knew generally where to look for game. At one point we came across the piles of manure from an apparent large herd of Cape buffalo. Yes, you can tell what type animal it is by their waste. One of the trackers stuck his finger in a pile to check the temperature. Yes he really did. He said they were fairly close and that we should continue on foot. We followed our tracker and the manure trail for perhaps a mile until we could see a number of Cape buffalo standing in a grove of acacia trees. We had circled so that we were 'down wind' of course — doesn't everyone know this. We approached slowly to within about 80 yards. You probably know that the Cape buffalo is quite a dangerous animal and is apt to charge. Since we were on foot, this kept crossing my mind. At this distance the tracker said we should take our best shot. I had brought a 275 hunting rifle from our compound and was ready. Even though I had hunted very little in the past, I had shot enough to realize that I was a pretty good shot with a rifle. I picked out a buffalo that was clear of the trees, steadied my rifle on a tree, took careful aim just behind the shoulder (at the heart), squeezed the trigger, and BOOM! You want to know what happened, don't you. The animal dropped in its tracks. That's right; it did! I had missed what I aimed at, but by serendipity the bullet struck the buffalo in the neck just behind the skull. The bullet probably severed the spinal cord. Of course I acted as if that was where I aimed. Beginner's luck! The workers immediately began to 'field dress' the animal, and quickly the meat was loaded into a pickup.

I shot my second Cape buffalo later as we were bouncing along in the back of the vehicle while following the running herd. Have you ever tried shooting when both you and your target are moving. Not easy. Well, I got lucky again. Boom! Oops; I forgot to tell Lou Ann that I was about to shoot. She was leaning out her side window not far from my rifle. I don't think her hearing has recovered yet. She says her tinnitus (ringing in the ears) began at that moment. I did wound the animal, for it was down. I must have hit it in the spine, for it couldn't use its hind legs. After finishing the animal, the workers again quickly did their job. As we were departing the area, I noticed that vultures were already beginning to descend on the remains. How quickly and efficiently nature's scavengers do their job.

As the day progressed, I shot an impala (our favorite meat) and a wart hog. I wounded the wart hog from our vehicle (stationary this time). It obviously was mortally wounded, so Bob and I approached it on foot. Bob had a 45 caliber pistol, and at close range he shot it in the head. (I'm sorry if you're squeamish about this). The bullet seemed to bounce off, and it just kept looking at us. Bob shot again. Same result. We were amazed! The third bullet finished the situation. By the way, the meat was delicious — much like roasted pig in America.

When we returned to Chimala, the meat was divided up among the missionary families, our co-workers, and the hunting safari workers. We claimed quite a bit of the Cape buffalo meat — including the ribs. Lou Ann had visions of delicious roasted and barbequed ribs. But NO!! We were totally unable to get them tender enough to eat — despite the best efforts of our cook, Zebron. We tried, but just think 'shoe leather'.

This was our one hunting trip in five years, and I haven't hunted since. But when I'm around people talking about their hunting prowess,

I just hold off for a while. Then I just quietly mention my "big game" hunting and the day I got two Cape buffalo, an impala, and a wart hog. Makes me seem like the "Mighty Hunter" — which I'm not. It sure gets people's attention though.

STORY OF FURAHINI MBAGO (BURNS)

"First meditate on Jesus, and then go out and look for Him in disguise."

– Mother Teresa

The story of Furahini speaks volumes about the differences in Tanznaia — as well as the USA. Furahini was a sixteen year old girl who suffered severe burns on both feet. She had a seizure disorder and had the misfortune of having a seizure while near an open fire (often fires were in their houses for heat during the cooler months). Many times others were afraid to help people in the midst of a seizure (convulsion). This has to do with the animistic belief that an evil spirit is causing it and would affect them if they touched the person. Furahini's Mother took her to the closest hospital, which happened to our government designated referral hospital in Mbeya. Because her family had little money, Furahini didn't have the benefit of seeing a doctor nor receiving even a modicum of decent burn care. Her care consisted of some occasional cleaning and dressing changes. There was no debridement of the burns (trimming off dead skin and tissue). This went on for almost a month. Her Mother realized that Furahini's feet were getting worse. To her everlasting credit she made the decision to take Furahini from the Mbeya hospital and bring her to us. Somehow she knew of our hospital.

I first saw Furahini one afternoon on female ward. What I first saw was a young girl who seemed terrified as she cowered from me. Both her feet were covered with very dirty, distorted bandages. What I haven't mentioned yet was the foul odor that greeted me even before I looked under the bandages — the odor of dead flesh and infection. I was afraid of what I might see as I was removing her dressings. My worst fears became reality as I looked at her feet. What I saw was necrotic (dead) skin and soft tissue. Bone was exposed in several areas. The foul pus was rampant and draining from the margins of her third degree burns. I was thinking, *"Oh my goodness; she's going to lose both her feet."* I tried not to look so disturbed and certainly didn't utter my thoughts in English or Swahili.

(I found out later that the reason Furahini seemed so terrified was because someone had told her that we were going to remove both her feet. Again, I never uttered my thoughts).

We began her treatment which consisted of daily cleaning, debridement, bandaging, and of course antibiotics. I had to clear up the infection and wait for the wounds to demarcate (the junction where dead tissue ended and the viable or live tissue began). This process would take about two weeks. It was clear that some amputation would be needed; I just couldn't know how much yet. During this time Furahini began to 'open up' as she got to know me better and realized we only wanted to help. She proved to be a very delightful and intelligent young lady. I can still see that coy smile.

It was always necessary to get permission for surgery — as it is in the USA. This was true even if it meant that death was almost a certainly without it. This happened all too frequently. So sad. I carefully explained to her mother what we needed to do — amputate some toes and put on skin grafts. She had to ask her husband for permission. In this male dominant culture the wife almost always acquiesces to her husband's decision. After waiting for nine days, Furahini's mother returned and signed the surgery permission form. In this interim Furahini's grandmother stayed with her.

During our first surgery I amputated her right little toe and the fifth metatarsal (the bone leading to the little toe). I did some skin grafting at this location and also some on her left foot. We had a Padgett's Dermatome (electrical instrument that shaves off skin at the proper thickness from a donor site, which is then applied to the needed area.). The donor site we used was from healthy skin on her thigh.

(Note: We had our Dermatome thanks to Dr. Danny Smelser who had brought it from the USA in 1993. He and Nancy and their three children were with us for a year. It was simply great having a compatriot doctor with whom to discuss cases and to share the work load.)

Her wounds and grafts healed well without infection — PTL! The bane of skin grafting was having infection occur. Infection would totally destroy the graft — almost as if it had melted off. It was always with guarded anticipation and a sense of dread as I removed the bandaging from grafts. In our environment it was most difficult to keep things sterile; and consequently, too many times the grafts "didn't take". It took so much time and work to care for burns; and when this happened, it all seemed so futile. I admit that I would also feel angry when this happened. Everything had to be repeated.

Furahini was a champ. She was a very cooperative patient; and became the joy of the female ward. She had lost all fear of me, and we could playfully joke when we made rounds. It did take a second surgery to finish more skin grafting, and these also did very well. As her grafts healed, she progressed so that she could wear shoes. Lou Ann gave her a pair of her tennis shoes. When she proudly walked around in her 'new shoes', you couldn't tell anything had ever happened.

Furahini is the type of case that makes it all so worthwhile. In a culture where disabilities are often discriminated against, we had given her a new lease on a normal life. Altogether she spent about two months in our hospital. Of course her family didn't have the money to pay her bill. Lou Ann and I quietly paid her bill when she left the hospital.

The story doesn't quite end here. I saw Furahini only one more time. About a month later as I was leaving my office, there was Furahini standing on the walkway — in Lou Ann's shoes. Without saying a word she smiled as she began unraveling the waist band of her wrapper or katanga — this is where women often kept their money. She then grasped some coins and extended them to me. I was really taken aback but took the coins, smiled (with a tear in my eye), and said "asante sana" (thank you very much). She continued smiling as she turned and walked away. Furahini was actually paying on her bill. Amazing and so touching. Like I said before; this is what makes it all worthwhile.

I'll add some words about burns in general. I've said many times that, _"I hate burns."_ They are very painful; they are nasty, dirty, and smelly; they take a long time; they are fraught with many complications; they are disfiguring. Having said that, I hasten to say that even though I hate burns, this is probably second only to obstetrics as to where I helped the most. Having the dermatome I mentioned allowed us to give better burn care, and subsequently we got more and more burn patients. So what developed for me was a paradox: An area of medicine I liked the least became an area where I did the most good. So despite the conflict, the result was most gratifying.

FANTASTIC SIGHTS

"God is a magnificent artist, with the world as a museum
displaying His handiwork."

While it's true that when on our compound we were virtually always on duty, we did manage to get away every few months. Usually these trips were to Dar es Salaam, the Capitol city, to get supplies or to pick up guests or both. We did manage to make a few "touristy" trips and visit game parks and the truly fantastic sights unique to Tanzania. These were Mount Kilimanjaro and the Ngorongoro Crater.

Mount Kilimanjaro rises out of the plains of northern Tanzania near Moshi to about 19,200 feet. It's an extinct volcano; and despite being only a few degrees south of the equator, it remains snow covered year round. But it's easily missed. What are you talking about? The mountain is so huge that it has its own ecosystem. The result is that quite frequently it's shrouded in clouds. You can spend several days in Moshi and never see the mountain — not even the hint of a mountain. And then, all of a sudden, the clouds can clear; and this huge, spectacular mountain looms forth in all its glory. Breathtaking! We've also had the privilege of flying over and around Kilimanjaro on a commercial flight from Nairobi to Dar. This is equally as spectacular from a totally different perspective.

Ngorongoro Crater: The very mention of its name stands alone. The Crater is indeed unique on the face of Planet Earth. There is absolutely nothing to compare. The Crater isn't far outside Arusha, Tanzania, and adjoins the Serengeti. It stands about 8,000 feet at the rim with the floor of the caldera some 2000 feet below. The diameter is some 14 miles — making it by far the largest caldera on the surface of Earth. The vastness is impossible to grasp. Due to the excellent grasses, the amount of rainfall, and its own water supply, it becomes the year round home to most types of African animals. There are a few types of animals that migrate out of the crater during certain seasons (elephants and wildebeests). We had the privilege of visiting the Crater on three occasions — each one as wondrous and spectacular as the proceeding. I should mention that I was able to drive our Land Cruiser down the wall of the Crater and all around the floor. A guide is necessary to properly navigate to the areas where game is most likely to be found. At times you find yourselves surrounded by hundreds of zebras, Cape buffalo, wildebeests, Thompson's gazelles, and many others. And yes, even lions at times. Speaking of lions. On one occasion we sat in our vehicle and watched the teamwork of several female lions sneaking up on some unsuspecting wildebeests. And then the chase began — spectacular to watch. You would never tire of visiting the Crater.

I know they are not in Tanzania; but I must include <u>Victoria Falls</u> on my list of "Fantastic Sights". These Falls are another of our Earth's natural wonders. We had the privilege of visiting the Falls on a road trip to a conference in Harare, Zimbabwe. The Falls are on the border between Zimbabwe and Zambia. They extend over about a mile in width as the waters of the Zambezi River plummet over the precipice into the chasm some 350 feet below. The amount of water is staggering — the most of any falls in the world. It's one of those few sights when you are filled with awe and rendered breathless. In a Newsletter article I said the Falls were indescribable. Then I proceeded in my lame attempt entitled, "Describing the Indescribable":

"It must be experienced. It is one of those times that silent awe is in order — not words. I am speaking of viewing Victoria Falls. They represent God's natural handiwork on the magnitude of the Grand Canyon. 'Mosi ya tunya' they are called — 'smoke that thunders.' The raging torrents of the Zambezi River plummet over a mile wide precipice into a narrow 350 foot abyss. The sheer volume of water, the magnitude of width and height, the mountainous boulders, the rising spray, the roar, the ever changing appearance, the rainbows — all these and more only begin to reveal one of God's great natural wonders on Earth."

Several years later we had the privilege of visiting Victoria Falls once again. The amazement and wonder were as fresh as our first visit. On this visit we were with a group of Harding University students for their semester in Zambia. Many of the students went bungee jumping from the bridge over the Zambezi River into the gorge below — the highest such jump in the world and certainly not for the faint of heart. Yes, I would have jumped also, but I thought better of it. Why? By now I had undergone a hip replacement and certainly didn't want a hip dislocation as the cord jerked you to a 'stop'. Instead I chose to take the whitewater rafting trip down the Zambezi. It is one of the roughest such rivers in the world — having many Class 5 rapids and some impassible areas where you have to portage. I had made several white-water trips and had some experience even with Class 5 rapids — the New River in West Virginia. We had some instruction first; but unfortunately, we had some first-timers with our group of six. I must say that it is imperative to listen to and immediately follow the instructions of the guide, who steers the raft. Don't even look; just paddle like crazy. Our very first rapids, as we put in the river not far below Victoria Falls, was a Class 5. Our guide was shouting the proper instructions as we approached the rapids, but our "newbies" were late and sluggish in following them. We hit the wall of water in the wrong position and were swamped — immediately capsizing. All our occupants, including our guide went flying into the swirling cauldron. That is, all but me. You see; our guide had said that *"No matter what, do not let go of the rope along the side of the raft"*. I didn't let go, but I found myself submerged underneath the overturned raft. Because of the force of the water, I couldn't pull myself over the raft's edge — in fact I was barely able to get my head above the water to breathe. There were definitely some moments of sheer terror and a real brush with death. Our guide saved me. He had been tossed out but somehow managed to get back to the raft. He climbed aboard our overturned raft, must have seen my hands on the rope, and helped pull me out of the water. The relief was overwhelming.

You might be wondering what happened to the other raft occupants. They were plucked from the water by the "safety crew". There were several men accompanying us in kayaks just for this purpose. I readily admit that after this harrowing experience, I had had enough! I "weenied out" and cringed quite low in the raft with each of the ensuing rapids. Fortunately, we didn't overturn again.

CHIMALA "TRAUMA CENTER"
("Planes, Trains, & Automobiles")

"I find He never guides us into an intolerable scramble of panting feverishness."

– Thomas Kelly

'll preface this chapter by telling you that prior to moving to Tanzania, I had worked for twelve years in an Emergency Department in a designated Level I Trauma Center (Methodist Hospital in Indianapolis, IN). I was actively involved in the initial care and stabilization of severe trauma patients. Needless to say, the contrast between Methodist and Chimala was like going back 50 years. Add to this the fact that we had no neurosurgery, orthopedic, plastic, or trauma surgery capabilities. Just me. I could basically handle the initial emergency presentations fairly well with our capabilities (or rather lack of capabilities), but then what? We did the best we could, but many patients suffered and died because of our deficits. Do I feel badly or guilty about this? At times. Why or why not? Because it was the best that could be done at that location at that time. There was no where else for the patients to go. I knew this and could accept it and move on to the next case. Does this sound hardened? I call it being adequately adjusted to and acceptant of our situation. This is the way I had to deal with these situations, so that I could give my full attention to the next patient. This was especially important in multiple trauma situations.

We had several horrible multiple trauma situations involving vehicle crashes. Sometimes we had as many as 25 injured patients from one accident. Most of the time there were also some fatalities at the scene. You probably have a mental picture of third world vehicles being very over loaded and crowded. Just imagine what happens when one of these vehicles crashes and overturns. Horrible carnage. At times like this, I resorted to true triage. Triage means the separating of patients according to type and severity of injury. The people with the most severe injuries who would probably not live were put aside. The severe ones that we could possibly help were treated first. The others would wait — the ones with simple fractures, lacerations, etc. I don't know how this sounds to you, but it is a tried and true method. It is especially needed in a situation like ours at Chimala.

The following is a Newsletter write-up I did after one of our major trauma situations. I entitled it, "*CHIMALA TRAUMA CENTER*":

"Oh, you haven't heard about us? We've just been added to the Official Register of Trauma Centers. Now if you believe this, I have grave doubts regarding your mental ability. But one Sunday recently we served as a trauma center for the thirteen wazungu (white people) injured in a tour truck accident. It overturned nearby when it struck an unlighted and unmarked stalled tractor in the road. As I approached the hospital entrance that night at 8:30 with Dr. Steve Smith for our routine night rounds, we were met by two young people limping along with one saying, "Is there a doctor around here?" I assured them that in the midst of their tragedy this was their lucky night. The first wave of casualties brought us the six in the worst condition. All of a sudden here I was back at Methodist Hospital's Trauma Center again. I triaged the cases with Steve and Tom (Dr. Pryor) — our two visiting doctors this month. We sewed wounds, splinted fractures, etc. Janice and Thobias (medical assistant) and some of our Nursing staff pitched in and did all the necessary things. All in all considering that we are a bush hospital, I think things went quite smoothly. Steve and I had to go to surgery with the Tanzanian man who was on the tractor. We opened his abdomen because of internal bleeding in addition to amputating his mangled left leg below the knee. He recovered nicely. (I relied heavily on Dr. Maurice King's book, <u>Primary Surgery, Volume 2 — Trauma</u>).

- To tell you the truth about the amputation, I had never done one or seen one. True! I went to my house and read the section in Dr. King's book on leg amputation (complete with illustrative pictures). Then I went to the hospital and performed the surgery.

That's right. "Wow", you say; "Isn't that dangerous, audacious, or foolhardy?" Remember that I was the only doctor available to do the procedure, and it was quite necessary. The old medical adage of, "See one; Do one; Teach one", didn't fit my case. Mine was more like: "Read about one; Go do it." With the willingness to do the procedure, following basic surgical techniques, and while following Dr. King's method, I didn't consider it risky or foolhardy.

- I'll also add to my Newsletter that even though the man's leg amputation healed well, he couldn't accept it. He became very depressed. Loss of a body part is just not accepted in their culture. The long term result?

How unusual it was to see wazungu as in-patients at Chimala! They were from the USA, England, and Australia. Probably a first. Seriously, these people were probably at the best possible place they could have been in the entire country of Tanzania. Three experienced USA doctors. What would I have done without you, Tom and Steve? The injured were evacuated to their respective countries.
[And yes, they actually went by train, plane, and automobile (bus) to Dar to get transport out of the country.]. *They kept Lou Ann and everyone busy with various needs — everything from food to clothes to toothbrushes to 'you name it.' WHEW! Also they couldn't believe it when their bills came to about $10.00 apiece. I'm sure these wazungu will never forget CHIMALA TRAUMA CENTER. *** As I always say, our greatest danger here is not some exotic tropical disease or snakebite; it's the roadway."*

A humorous side light occurred involving one of the young men who was injured. He was on the male ward along with 19 others. He needed to urinate but said he couldn't go with all the people around. He didn't want to go in the Male Ward bathroom — which was more than a little bit odoriferous. *"Pull the roll away partition around him,"* I said. Still he said he couldn't go. Janice had sympathy on him, gave him a bottle, and directed him to her office where he took care of his business.

DOCTOR; "CHANGED CONDITION"

"Communication; all is communication."

I instituted a system whereby the nurse in charge would write certain information about a patient on a form. Then the student, guard, or other 'runner' would bring the note to the Medical Assistant or Doctor on-call. The form was quite simple; just requiring their name, new patient or current in-patient, what ward, the problem, the vital signs, and the condition. The condition had three categories: Serious (see immediately), Intermediate, and Minor. One thing for sure — when the note said, _"Changed Condition"_, I had to go and quickly. This phrase means something totally different at Chimala than in your local hospital. I found out it was really synonymous with near death or impending death. I'll share with you a sampling of the information on some forms I received from the nurses:

- Problem: *"Rupture case"*. This turned out to be an evisceration (an abdominal stab wound resulting in the intestines protruding)
- Problem: *"Got cut wound on the noise"*
- Problem: *"In dying stage with big abscess"*
- Problem: *"Please doctor; we have problem in Female Ward about the patient of meningitis — the drip broken so we ask your help."* — Translated this means there's trouble with the IV (they called IV's a "drip" there)
- Problem: *"Patient pail"*
- Problem: *"General body weakness and sharrow in breathing."* — In case you didn't figure it our; that's <u>shallow</u> breathing
- Problem: *"Please come to see patient on OB ward — got placenta retained and the cord cut out."*
- Problem: *"Kindly come down to Male Ward. We have a patient who have been knocked by a car."* ("Knocked" is synonymous with our "hit".)

- Problem: *"Patient in changed condition. Is unable to talk."*
- Problem: *"Please come to see patient on Female Ward. Pulse nil."* ("Nil" of course means not present)
- Problem: *"Please, I have emergency case in OB — Eclampsia — she had fits X2 at home and X1 here."*

These notes were minimally helpful, but basically I didn't know what I was dealing with until I arrived on the scene. That's the bottom line. No matter the time of day or what I was doing, I had to go. As I've written, one of the hallmarks of Third World medicine is delayed presentation. I didn't want to further delay a patient's care by not being prompt.

"OFF TIME"

"There is nothing wrong or unnatural with feeling weary, but there is everything wrong with abandoning the ship in the midst of the fight."

This title is a bit of a misnomer; for as long as I was on the compound, I was never really off. Multiple trauma cases, severe medical emergencies, consults, or simply the volume of patients would find me summoned to the hospital — even when I was ostensibly 'off-call'. "What am I here for anyway?" Without question I always went when called. I'm no martyr; this is only as it should be.

My physical exercise and 'mental escape' were both accomplished in my eight mile bike rides four to five days a week. I loved the solitude, but somehow I was still available. On two occasions someone from the hospital came by vehicle and intercepted me. You got it; they needed me at the hospital.

Aside: An unexpected and unwanted result of my rides was when young teenage boys would come out to ride with me. But they weren't really there to ride with me. They were there to challenge the 'mzee' (old man — by then 55 years old). They knew my route and would jump ahead of me while frequently looking back. This was definitely a challenge to beat me to the end of my ride. I should interject here that my multiple-geared mountain bike had a distinct advantage over their very heavy single-geared Chinese made bikes — even if I did have 35-40 years on them. Only once did someone almost beat the old man. Usually I would easily take them on the one mile steady incline not long before the finish. On this one day I think they sent out their village champion to finally take me. He jumped in early on the final incline and gave the 'challenge look' as he increased his speed. I vigorously tried not to let him get further ahead; but alas, he did. Had I finally met my match? As my thighs were increasingly burning, I had to just back off and recover a bit. As we neared the summit of the incline, he had about fifty yards on me. Oh well, so I surrender being the Chimala champion. I noticed that he kept looking back but did so more infrequently. In the intervening minutes my thighs had almost recovered, and I thought that perhaps with some strategy at the end I could take him. I had seen bicycle races in the velodrome when the rider behind the leader seems to have the advantage. So my strategy was that about two hundred yards from the end, I would 'take off' as fast as I could — the very instant after his glance. It worked. I charged; and by the time of his next glance, I was already about to overtake him. Too late for him to accelerate. I blew by him about fifty yards from the end. Victory! — See what I mean. A temporary physical and mental release from the sadness and tragedies at the hospital.

Of course we did have hours of no clinical responsibility. (I should tell you here that Lou Ann was also always on-call for any needs or problems in her areas of supervision.). What did we do? Remember, we had no television capability and none of the American amenities such as movie theaters, concerts, museums, sporting events, nice restaurants, malls, etc. Frankly, we didn't miss most of these. We did read a lot. I think I read about 75 Louis La'Mour westerns — all that we could get. I read all the non-fiction books in probably fifty Reader's Digest condensed books. I think Lou Ann read all the books — fiction and non-fiction. We did have a television set with VCR capability (Video Cassette Recording — for those of you who don't remember these). This gave us the ability to see movies and recordings of families, sporting events, television shows, etc. Steve, my son-in-law, faithfully recorded Indiana University basketball games which I thoroughly enjoyed. (I appreciated fast-forwarding past the time-outs and commercials.). Of course I didn't know who had won the games until I saw them. An added bonus was that IU was outstanding in this era.

Then there were the doldrums of dry season when it was quite hot; and you couldn't imagine the countryside being drier, browner, or uglier. Sometimes during this season we drove around simply to enjoy the pleasure of being cool — in our air conditioned Land Cruiser.

On one such Saturday afternoon our 'entertainment' was watching Janice's new water bed fill up with the trickle from the hose. Yes, believe it or not, sometimes things got a bit boring.

One thing I faithfully did every month was to write our Newsletter — called "Perspectives". This was our one link to the 'outside world', so that the recipients would get a taste of our lives. I would type the Newsletter either on a computer or an honest to goodness real typewriter — when the computer 'went down'. I kept log books in my office to document cases, situations, thoughts, and perspectives. This process in itself was a bit 'therapeutic'. I always made two copies of the Newsletter and mailed one to my daughter and one to our church — in separate envelopes. This was my attempt to circumvent any glitches in the postal service. Copies were then made in the USA to send to those on our mailing list.

A huge event each month was 'phone day'. On one Saturday per month at a designated time and number, various ones would call us. We received our calls at a motel in Mbeya (a two hour round trip drive from our home). We would eat lunch there, go to a designated room, and hopefully receive our calls. (Janice came to receive her calls also). No matter how many times we did this, there always seemed to be confusion. I would write down my name, who would be calling, and to put the call through to the designated room. Sound simple? My daughter, Melanie, would usually be calling first; and if she got through, she'd hear Swahili or perhaps some English with an African accent. She would say she was calling for "Black". She would hear; "Who?", "What?", "Black?" "Who?" By persistence she would be patched through to us. I should tell you here that the rule was to keep trying to call for thirty minutes. If you couldn't get through, then the next one designated to call would give it a go. The reason the calls came from the USA to Tanzania was because it was much cheaper. Sometimes our callers would hear, *"The Indian Ocean satellite is out of position."* Or it might be, *"The country is busy."* At any rate, needless to say, these calls were so very important to us. A real downer day was the trip back to Chimala when the calls had not come through. (Just compare this to our current missionaries who have immediate access at all times wherever they are — with their international telephone service, Skype, and the myriad of other services.)

A few times when I was off for the weekend we both might really need to get away for a day or so. Sometimes we went to the Baptist Guest House in Iringa which was only about an hour an a half away. Even though quite Spartan, it provided some meals and our needed respite. Iringa was situated high on a mountainous ridge and originally had been a German town — being a bit cooler and more free of mosquitoes. We had a couple trips to guest houses on Lake Malawi, which was about two hours away. Lake Malawi is a Rift Valley lake — quite narrow and deep — and separates Tanzania from Malawi. One trip was on the Tanzanian side and another on the Malawian side. On this latter trip I did something I said I'd never do! I paid a bribe. I can't remember the specific circumstances, but I just remember being particularly stressed and fatigued and just had to get away. At the border the Malawian guards had me convinced that I couldn't get by. Something about paperwork on my Land Cruiser. It always seems that you can get 'one-upped' by the ubiquitous paper work. Anyway, one guard said, "Come with me". This is usually the cue that he wants to get you alone with a chance of getting a bribe. They never use the 'bribe' word or discuss it with their co-workers. When we were alone, I uttered the tell-tale words, *"What must I do?"* This is the signal to him that I'm willing to consider paying a bribe. At this point some gesture or mention of money is apparent. By the way, bribery like most everything else, is subject to bargaining. I can't even remember what I gave him, but soon we were on our way across the border.

There was another time when we really wanted to get away for a night. This time we thought we'd just go to Mbeya and stay in the hotel where we received our phone calls. Mistake! And I'll tell you why. When we checked in, we realized there were no mosquito nets (a must in our malaria infested environment). It gets worse. The window coverings had small holes in them and no screens. Soon after going to sleep we began to be dive-bombed by countless mosquitoes. Oh well, we'll just sleep with our heads covered by the sheets. Of course this made the situation hotter and more uncomfortable and eventually unbearable. After a few hours, our mutual decision was to get up and go back to Chimala where at least we had mosquito protection. Wow, what a wonderful time away we had!

When we had guests, we tried to take them to Kimani Falls. These Falls were high in the rugged mountains not far from Chimala. A voluminous amount of water cascaded down a series of rocky cliffs. In the USA this area would be a National Monument if not a National Park. That's how magnificent the Falls are. When Lou Ann's parents, Kermit and Ruby Brantly, and my sister-in-law, Joanne Black, visited us in 1993, we were looking for something scenic to do on a Friday afternoon. This was because Ruby had asked, "What do you do for fun on Friday afternoons?" Off to Kimani Falls we went. I need to tell you that the last half of the trip has no road. That's right. You make your own way up the steep, rocky mountainside. And yes, a four-wheel drive is a must. We reached the summit and were enjoying the Falls when one of those sudden rainy season torrents struck. So back down we went. What were dry slopes and stream beds on our ascent became wet and slippery slopes and raging streams on our descent. It really posed no difficulty for our trusty Land Cruiser. In fact as the driver, it was rather fun. I can't say the same for my mother-in-law, who was just short of terrified. She used a memorable phrase that we will never forget — *"I'm never going to ask again what you do for fun on Friday afternoon."*

BLESSING OF LOCATION // VICTIM OF LOCATION

"Never give in, never give in; never, never, never, never ——
in nothing, great or small, large or petty —— never give in,
except to convictions of honor and good sense."
– Winston Churchill

N ever forget that in our yet imperfect USA we have the very best that is currently available in medical care. This care is available to you no matter where you are and regardless of your ability to pay — twenty-four hours a day. If a real emergency situation occurs, you will get the proper care — period. Never forget this. You have the *"Blessing of Location."* Now compare this to Third World medicine or in our world of missionary medicine. Here you are the *"Victim of Location."* Frequently the care is simply not available — period. Third World doctors, besides often being poorly qualified, are often too few and far between. Much of the equipment that is standard in the USA is not available.

Let me give some examples of the "Blessing of Location". I observed all these on just one Sunday morning at our church when home on leave. As I looked around the audience, I saw these people who, had they lived in the Third World, would probably have died.

- Mary England suffered a cardiac arrest at her home. She was saved by her son-in-law, who knew CPR, and the paramedics.
- Rob Harris had coronary artery obstruction at the origin of the left main coronary artery (this is called the "widow maker"). He had angioplasty (the "rotor-rooter" procedure) and is doing great.
- David Smith survived a ruptured cerebral aneurysm with neuro-surgery.
- Evelyn Cole also survived a ruptured cerebral aneurysm with neurosurgery. (Both David and Evelyn are doing very well after surgery).

- Erin Gentry is a ten year survivor of osteogenic sarcoma (bone cancer) of her femur.
- Lucy Artis is a ten year survivor of cancer of the thyroid.
- Linda Richards is doing well after long-term treatment for cancer of the colon.
- Aaron Butler is back to normal after a near fatal infectious disease with sepsis.

Amazing, isn't it! All these cases in just one morning at church. And these are just the ones I recognized with fatal or potentially fatal emergency conditions. It doesn't begin to count the number of people who've had cataract surgery, prosthetic joints, cardiac by-pass surgery, and a myriad of other surgical procedures or treated medical conditions.

Where we live and work in Tanzania, there is no neurosurgery or cardiac surgery available. There are no oncologists, no joint replacement, no neonatology, and the list goes on and on. This is one of the most difficult areas with which to deal. Unavailability. I know exactly what could be done if — if only the patients were elsewhere. No, I cannot do all these procedures. Even if I could, we don't have the staff, the equipment, and all the ancillary needs for these procedures. So what happens? They don't get the needed treatment. No, it's just not possible to send all these cases needing specialty care to proper locations. Why? — logistics, time, money, patients' desire, etc. So what do I do? I do the best we can at Chimala with our capabilities and limitations and try not to think about what could be.

A few other very significant facts also show the stark difference in our two cultures:
1. When we moved to Tanzania, the life expectancy there was 51. Actually it probably decreased after that because of HIV/AIDS. Comparatively the life expectancy in the USA is over 75.
2. About one in four children die before the age of five.
3. Virtually everyone has chronic malaria.

I don't want to end this chapter on such a sour note. You must never forget that we indeed do a lot of good. By far the most common things we see and treat are the most common. What do I mean? The disease entities most common here comprise by far the majority of what we see: malaria, dysentery, pneumonia, skin infections, burns, parasitic disease, obstetrics, minor trauma, etc. For the most part we can do a very good job of treating these and other entities. We don't compare ourselves with the USA of course. Our comparison is with other hospitals of similar size and location in Tanzania. When we do this, we are consistently ranked near the top.

MEDICAL ETHICS AT CHIMALA

"Do not pray for easy lives; pray to be stronger people. Do not pray for tasks equal to your powers; pray for power equal to your tasks."

– P. Brooks

What is right or wrong (ethical or unethical) is not a set of guidelines that are applicable in all locations and at all times. Ethics changes; yes it does. The factors that alter this fact are timing, availability, setting, choices, personnel and training, supplies and equipment, patient expectation, cultural experience and capability, and others. I'll give some situations I faced in decision making at Chimala. Keep asking yourselves what you would do. Were my decisions right or wrong (ethical or unethical)? And why?

- Use of antibiotics: Use of the expensive, high-powered American antibiotics was reserved for those with serious infectious diseases and with a 'chance' of recovery. Some patients' infections would just be too far advanced. In these cases we often had to decide on whom to use these antibiotics — especially purchased and sent from the USA but limited in amount. We simply did not have enough to use on everyone. Usually we decided to use them on children and their parents, post-op patients, burns, obstetrics, and certain resistant infections. They typically were not used on routine minor cases or hopeless patients (such as advanced HIV/AIDS). But please understand that we did not withhold care from anyone. On these latter cases we did use antibiotics. It's just that we used the ones we could purchase in country.

- HIV/AIDS: At the time we were in Tanzania [1992-97], HIV/AIDS was a proverbial death sentence. There were no antiviral meds available. I didn't see a single AZT tablet in my years there. Consequently, I chose not to do any elective surgery on these patients (elective cases are not emergencies but are surgeries that could wait indefinitely). Can you possibly imagine refusing elective surgery in America? Simply stated; the HIV/AIDS patients were not going to live. Another fact about surgery in these patients was that they were very prone to postoperative infections. Early in my time at Chimala and before I started HIV testing before surgery, I would find out after the fact why these patients got infected.

Of course we did the necessary C-sections on HIV(+) mothers. There was no certainty that the children would have HIV/AIDS — even though in that environment the percentage was around 60%, if you added in the risk from breast feeding. When faced with a life or death emergency surgery, we would do the surgery. But I must confess that I silently prayed that such patients would not come in on my watch.

- Oxygen: We usually only had one tank of oxygen and one delivery system. We would have to make a judgment on which patient needed it the most. By necessity we had to exclude the patients who were basically hopeless — this included the HIV/AIDS patients. A note on oxygen: At one time we went five months without any oxygen. There was some problem in Dar es Salaam in receiving a shipment. Add this to my list of _"What is Third World?"_

- Simultaneous C-sections: Two women needing C-sections were there at same time. Both were showing severe fetal distress. We could only do one at a time (one doctor; one operating room; one surgical team). Remember, there was no hospital within an hour's drive; and of course there was no assurance our patient would be quickly attended if she did get there. At the very quickest it would be an hour before we could get to the second woman. Which one to do first? I chose the woman who had no living children. Two others had died at delivery — because she needed a C-section and didn't have one (at another hospital). The other woman had living children at home. The woman I operated first had a very healthy baby. After surgery I quickly checked the other woman. Her baby had died in utero (in the uterus before it could be delivered). Choices have to be made. This situation did not pose a problem at Chimala. Can you only imagine if such a situation happened in the USA?

Were these decisions difficult? Of course they were, but practicality had to reign. Having no options did somewhat ease the decision making in our setting. I hope I don't sound crass and uncompassionate. I certainly took the decisions seriously. No, I didn't "play God". We were in a situation that necessitated such decisions. It's just the way it is there. (I refer you to the section on, *"Blessing of Location" versus the "Victim of Location".*)

Ethical Questions for you to ponder:

- First a general question: <u>Aren't medical ethics the same everywhere</u> in every circumstance?

- <u>Do you transfer a child from Chimala to a facility that can correct a congenital heart defect?</u>
A child has a fully treatable heart defect that requires surgery. They are in heart failure and don't have long to live. What do you do? Do you make it a project to raise the funds and go through the extensive process of trying to get the child to a capable surgical facility? (Johannesburg, Europe, USA). Remember, there are many other cases requiring some type specialized care. Do you choose this child? Why? Why do you not choose all the others? You can readily see how these dilemmas can become overwhelming.

- Do you pass out condoms to all comers in the clinic to "prevent" HIV/AIDS?

First of all condoms are not 100% effective in prevention of HIV/AIDS. During our tenure in Tanzania the diagnosis of HIV was essentially a death sentence. There was no definitive treatment available. Are you giving a false sense of security by dispensing them? Are you encouraging indiscriminate sex? Of course you are assuming they will be used properly. Some men refused to use them.

- When someone is literally dying from blood loss, do you give them blood from someone when their HIV status is unknown?

Remember that the incidence of HIV in our community was about 20% among the 15-50 age range. To answer my own question, we have given unknown status blood in extremely critical situations. This was a rare situation, for we had quick HIV tests available that only took a few minutes.

- Do you use out-of-date drugs when no others are available?

I will answer this question for you — yes, yes, and yes! You should know there is nothing 'magic' about the expiration date. It is a relative date set because the drug manufacturer is required to place an expiration date. Stated in a more scientific way; this date may represent when the medicine has lost perhaps 20% of its effectiveness. You see; it's not even a question worth considering. I will quickly add that to the Tanzanians the expiration date was the END ALL and BE ALL. If you gave a medicine even one day past the expiration date, it was anathema — as if you were poisoning the patient. I tried to explain that medically speaking the medications were still good. I told them that we used these medicines on ourselves. All our explanations were futile. The Ministry of Health had stated that 'out-of- date' medicines should not be used. This became like a "decree from God."

Occasionally an Official unannounced group would show up and inspect our pharmacy for out-of-date medicines. To show you how ridiculous it was; one time we were cited for an out of date laxative! Medicines coming in the country were supposed to not be within six months of the expiration date. This posed quite a problem because we could buy 'short-dated' medicines much cheaper. Consequently, my wife (head of pharmacy) became most adept at changing labels, changing packaging, changing bottles, hiding medicines, etc.

- Do you use chloramphenicol (chloromycetin)?
This is an older but good antibiotic with a broad spectrum of bacterial coverage. One problem: it causes an irreversible aplastic anemia in about 1 in 25,000 people. Because of this fact, it has not been used in the United States since the 60's. It is available and rather inexpensive in Tanzania. Would you use it in Tanzania? I did. I will add that in my years in Africa there was one case where I might have seen this complication.

- Do you do elective surgery on HIV positive patients?
[I discussed this in another section]

- Do you withhold mother's breast milk from her baby if she's HIV positive?
First of all, we don't know at this stage if the infant has contracted HIV from mother. HIV can be transmitted via breast milk in up to 20% of babies. It is totally cultural for mothers to breast feed. To try and tell mothers otherwise is futile. Milk formulas are hard to come by and are expensive. Now you know the answer. In some desperate situations where breastfeeding mothers were too sick to produce milk, we tried to introduce the "wet nurse" concept — have another lactating woman feed their baby. For some reason this was not acceptable in their culture.

- Do you turn away patients who are untreatable?

  This depends totally on the case. Example: Rabies is virtually 100% fatal once symptoms appear. There is no treatment. Plus, it can be transmitted from one person to another. On two occasions I have sent patients with rabies home to die. I explained the situation to their relatives and said there was nothing that could be done. I should add that other patients (and staff) in the hospital were extremely afraid of being around the affected person.

  In the USA if we cannot personally help a patient, it becomes our responsibility to properly refer them. Most often this is just not possible in Tanzania. Rarely were there consultants capable of helping. Some examples would be late stage cancer and severe orthopedic or other deformities.

- What do you tell a woman who is HIV negative, her husband is HIV positive, yet he refuses to use a condom?

  Remember, this is a male dominant culture; and women have little say. The husband is likely to cast her out if she refuses him. If this does happen, her family may not take her back. In letting her husband have his way, it's just a matter of time until she becomes HIV positive. She has little choice.

- Do you charge fees to patients who have no money?

  Being a missionary hospital we took on all comers. We treated everyone the same (I did mention a few of the necessary exceptions). Fees were charged, but the treatment received was not related to payment. Also we had no differential payment scale — whether it was a wealthy merchant from Mbeya or a Masaai goat herder from the bush. Most people were faithful in trying to pay their bill. A few would pay off the bill "in kind" by doing some type work around the hospital. Our financial officer, being a Tanzanian, would work through the village leaders. They knew who could and couldn't pay. It would often be surprising how money would suddenly show up. If indeed they could not pay, then it was 'written off.'

The "dependency syndrome" always has to be guarded against. It's possible in all people everywhere. Africans are not excluded. If you give people something for nothing, they often expect the same or more next time — and the next. It's human nature. It's also 'contagious' — *"If so and so got it, then why not me?"* People need "ownership" of their medical care or any project helping them. If they have a stake in something, they're much more likely to care, to work, or to pay. (See my chapter on "Fostering Dependency")

- Should I do some procedure that I've never done before?
  I've gone into this elsewhere, but I'll give the short answer. Being a "bush hospital" we were isolated, and I was the most trained medical person available. Perhaps a better question than the above would be, *"Should I let a patient suffer and possibly die rather than trying to help?"* My conclusion was that if I had more of a chance of helping than hurting the patient, I proceeded. Ethically this was right in my location. Ethically it would be wrong in the USA. Therefore, medical ethics are relative.

- Infertility Work-ups:
  I'll preface this section by reiterating that the various tribes in Africa are male dominant. I'm not being judgmental — just stating the way it is. An outgrowth of this is the value placed on having male children. Many people there still don't know that the sex of the child is determined by the father's XY chromosome. Not understanding this leads to the man often putting his wife aside for not having a male child. The wives are even more likely to be put aside for not being able to have any children at all. Of course this also can be due to the man.

  The most unhappy married women in Tanzania were the ones who were unable to have children. As I've said, the man most often thought it was her fault. In order to try and solve the dilemma unfortunately we were only capable of a few things at Chimala. We could do sperm counts. We could do simple gynecologic exams to see if the woman's anatomy was normal. This was about it. These having been done and if things were normal, I would tell the couples to keep trying and praying.

I also had another group of couples who came in for "infertility problems." In this group the woman had not been able to have any recent children. She may have had one or two children soon after marriage, but no pregnancies in several years. If the woman's current husband was the father of the children she had, we made the assumption that his sperm count was sufficient. And because she was able to previously have children, we knew that her system was adequate. What I am leading up to is that I had nothing else to offer these couples in our setting. I would tell them that God had given them a child (our children) and to be the best Christian parents they could. I reminded them that another pregnancy was possible.

I never felt good about how I handled these situations (or better yet didn't handle them). My approach had to do with our location. Ethically, this would not be appropriate in most other settings. So once again, what is "right" or "ethical" in one setting would not be in a different setting. Another example of ethics being relative — based on location, time, culture, religion, supply, personal beliefs, patient requests, and other factors.

- Tubal Ligation:
  I had a very sad case that needed a C-section. This teenaged girl was quite mentally retarded and had been sexually molested. She was unable to deliver the child. An even worse part I haven't told you is that this was her second pregnancy — and C-section. She had been repeatedly abused. The C-section proceeded well and the baby looked normal. The standard procedure if a tubal ligation has been requested is that it is done at the conclusion of the C-section. Normally the woman expresses her desire for the

procedure and signs the operative form. This girl probably functioned at the level of a three year old — rendering her unable to understand much less sign a form. I had considered her situation prior to the C –section and had decided to do a tubal ligation. One of the nurses in the room said, *"You can't do that; she hasn't signed."* I said quickly that she was unable to sign as I continued with the ligation. What do you think? Ethical or unethical? The procedure may never have happened if I'd tried to get a form signed by her parents. Unknown.

- CPR:
  You all know what CPR stands for in the USA (CardioPulmonary Resuscitation). It's performed when either the heart is not functioning (no pulse or heart tones) or a person is not breathing. It's performed in most medical situations in the hospital or by medics on the scene. So many are taught rudimentary CPR in the USA — from boy scouts to most public workers. We even have monitor/defibrillators in most public places. To perform CPR in a sudden arrest situation is a given. What would you think if I told you I never did CPR in Tanzania? *"What?"* — *"I can't believe it,"* — *"That's malpractice."* Let me tell you of our situation before you decide I was unethical. We had no monitors; no defibrillators; no ventilators. Most patients who are successfully resuscitated are on a ventilator for some time. Once again, we had no ventilators. Most of our patients who died had been severely ill and had already received the maximum treatment we could give. There was nothing else we could do. The secret to successful resuscitation even in the USA is immediacy — this means starting resuscitation within 3-5 minutes. If it is begun after that and even if the patient survives, there is usually substantial brain damage. Without monitors and close observation at Chimala, we lost the advantage of immediacy. Perhaps now you can see why CPR was a useless exercise for us. What are your thoughts now? Ethical or unethical?

CHIMALA SCENARIO
(Typical Saturday?)
[This comes from one of my Newsletters]

"We are all faced with a series of great opportunities brilliantly disguised as impossible situations."

Well, here it is Saturday morning at 8AM, and I'm walking the one hundred yards from my house to the hospital — from the calm to the storm. You never know what awaits you. And how! Boy, I sure hope to have *an* easy, peaceful day. I'm tired...... Is that eight or nine C-sections in the last five days? The C/S I finished at 1:30 this morning was a hard one. The baby's head was really wedged in the mother's pelvis. Wow, was the family happy after I finished! It was because the mother has had five pregnancies but no living children. [As a physician, these are the special times of gratification.]. The four children she delivered all died within the first two months — two delivered at home and two at the Government hospital. She probably had prolonged labors with the result that the babies were quite depressed. Her pelvis was just too small. She should have had C-sections the other times. Thank God they decided to come here last night. We got surgery underway in only forty-five minutes — very good for us in the middle of the night. Obadiah was the night guard, and he hustles the best he can on his bicycle to get the operating team from their homes. The baby did just great — started crying right away as I was taking him from the uterus. I love it when that happens. Yes, it was a boy! The family was bowing, kneeling, smiling, and praising me. As always when people did this, I quickly added, *"Sifu Mungu, Mpozi ni Mungu."* ("Praise God; God is the real physician.").

Uh oh; What's that? Just inside the hospital gate and outside OB I see a woman lying on the walkway with the usual crowd around. Oh my goodness, she's convulsing. Looks like she's pregnant. Upon getting her into OB she is indeed a term pregnancy and in early labor. Her B.P is

220/120, and she's still unconscious. Looks like she's starting to seize again. It's an obvious case of eclampsia. "Margaret, let's get an IV started and give her 10mg IV valium and 10mg of apresoline. What do you mean you have no apresoline? Aren't you supposed to keep four vials on OB? They're empty! Why weren't they replaced? Where's Lou Ann; someone get Lou Ann." She'll get me some.

An hour has gone by. I've gotten Rehema's blood pressure down and her seizures have stopped. Surgery is getting assembled for her C-section. During this short time before surgery I needed to check on some in-patients. Today our census is 110 patients in our 89 bed hospital. Poor Janice has 47 kids on pediatrics and only 18 beds. I thought I'd better go to Pediatrics to see if I could help Janice. But first — what's on female ward? Let's see; I need to take the dressing off Tumaini's skin graft. I operated on her five days ago. Let me take a look — easy does it as I take off the dressing. Oh no; the left arm grafts look infected and almost half of them have sloughed off. How much more can she take? This was her third grafting procedure. She had third degree burns over about 50% of her body. What's that? Is that what I think it is crawling our from under her bandage? Yes it is; there are many of them. At least maggots don't harm the live tissue.

"Dr. Black; Dr. Black!" Yes Henry. (Henry is a nurse from surgery). He tells me the National Power is off. No problem Henry; just use the little generator for surgery. Let me know as soon as she's in the theatre (they used the British term for operating room).

What's all this blood on the sidewalk? Well, I know where it leads. I'd better go to minor theatre and check it out. What happened? It seems that two bicyclists collided. One patient is on male ward and is unconscious. The young man in minor sustained a severe through and through lower lip laceration. One of my medical assistants, Mwingira, tells me that he's already taken care of it. As I look at his completed suture job, it's quite apparent that he's sewed the lip crooked. It's just unacceptable. I could do a better job while blindfolded. Later after surgery I'll have to tear down his repair and do it properly. [I did that by the way and it looked much better]

I'll run by Pediatrics quickly. Janice has just gotten in an 18 month old girl that she thinks has meningitis. It's difficult to tell the difference between this and cerebral malaria. Both cause unconsciousness and seizures. As I did the spinal tap, we saw the terrible, disgusting looking, thick, cloudy spinal fluid. MENINGITIS! This is an example of another case that was brought in too late. We see so many like this. So sad. The families just don't know any better. By the way, Janice says; "After the C-section, you need to see this other little boy — looks like another femur fracture. It's just like the other two we've admitted this week". Where do they all come from? This little guy fell out of a mango tree.

Dr. Black; they're ready in surgery. I'm coming. "Janice, can you come over in a few minutes and help with resuscitation of the baby". It's already in a depressed condition. As I scurry off to surgery, a smartly dressed, smiling Tanzanian man approaches me and greets me in very good English. He introduces himself as being from the Ministry of Health. Being somewhat taken aback by my apparent confusion, he says, "Didn't you get our letter?" What letter? It seems a letter of intro-duction was again lost in our uncertain postal system. He says he's here to speak to the Medical Director (that's me) and ask some questions regarding our hospital. I told him I was quite sorry, but we didn't receive the letter. I added that I was on my way to surgery for a dire emergency. I spotted Janice across the way and quickly told her the situation — hop-ing that she could appease him. I dashed for surgery.

"Where's Mwingira"? Our Medical Assistants usually assist in surgery. "He can't come". "Why not"? "He's alone in clinic". "Why"? "Where's Thobias"? Not back from leave yet. He was supposed to start back yesterday. "Have you heard from him"? No, of course not. Clinic is backed up, so Mwingira will have to stay there. "Rainer; you can assist me. Don't worry; you'll do fine". (Rainer is our scrub nurse). So here we are with a full blown OB emergency — with mother and baby in grave danger, short staffed, no proper assistant, no oxygen, and me. Is there anything else that can go wrong? Oops! I shouldn't have said it. Remember, Murphy was Tanzanian. As I'm scrubbing for surgery (in brown river water), I'm silently praying that God will help me forget everything else so that I can focus all my thoughts and energies on this surgery. As my prayer is lingering in my thoughts, Henry comes running in and says, "Hamna petrol." "What? Why"? He has said that there is no fuel for the small generator. Remember; no National Power. Now no power at all. Of course we need electricity for our lights and suction. Is someone supposed to keep the fuel can supplied? Certainly. TIA strikes again. Lou Ann — get Lou Ann. She'll have to run get some petrol (gasoline) from the station. I must go ahead and start the case (I keep extra flashlights available for just such times).

As always I started surgery with a prayer, but this time with a special emphasis: "Tunaomba kwamba utawasaidia Rehema, na mtoto wake, na mimi." (I was asking God to help the mother, child, and me!). Lou Ann did get the petrol and got the generator started just at the critical juncture of the operation. Actually the case turned out quite well — despite our rocky beginning. Meanwhile Bahati (our 'float nurse') performed some of her usual duties. These included killing the flies that very accurately kept dive bombing us and wiping the sweat off my face and glasses before drops would cascade into our operative field.

Indeed we are "fearfully and wonderfully made" by our Creator. Rehema was no exception. She did great during surgery and afterwards. Her baby was somewhat depressed at birth but recovered nicely. Praise the Lord.

The account of this one morning clearly depicts what missionary medicine is like in a Third World bush hospital.

"LABOR OF LOVE" — (OB-OB-OB)

"We are here to add what we can to, not get what we can from life."

– Sir William Osler

There were two distinct areas that drove me crazy at the hospital. Actually they were like a double-edged sword — causing extreme ambivalence. I liked both areas and didn't like them — all at the same moment. Why didn't I like them and what were they? They were disruptive, demanding, time insensitive, time consuming, messy, and more. On the positive side, these areas caused me more satisfaction than any others at the hospital. Confusing enough for you? The areas were Obstetrics and Burn Care. These two entities are rather polar opposites in most regards. As I describe the care of burns elsewhere, you'll see why this was simultaneously a chore but ultimately an area of great satisfaction. I guess I didn't like the process but liked the result. Obstetrics was also a love-hate relationship — for an entirely different reason. When I mentioned 'time insensitive', there is nothing that rivals Obstetrics. The only thing routine about OB is that it has no routine. But oh my, how it can disrupt your days — and nights! Thus the term "Love-Hate" for OB. Who likes to be unpredictably but regularly awakened at night and ready to respond immediately? When I was on-call, my last thought before drifting into sleep would be a prayer that I would awaken quickly and respond appropriately if called — and be nice. Yes, I had some trouble with this. Just ask Lou Ann. Dr. Henry Farrar, a long-time medical missionary and good friend calls OB the "snake pit". I used this term as well as the "shark pool" and other terms of endearment.

The reason for my dual feelings about these two situations has to do with the results. I often had the all too human feelings of futility and fatigue or success and failure. Janice uses the term "bittersweet" to describe not just these situations but Third World medicine in general. But these feelings were superseded by good results and the resultant patient satisfaction. To see healthy, happy, active babies and burn patients made everything else worthwhile. Looking at the totality of my medical work at Chimala, I'm sure I saved more lives through Obstetrical care than through all other areas combined (mothers and babies).

OBSTETRICS

I'll write more about OB even though I've done so elsewhere. After all, time-wise no other service even compares. Hours and hours and night after night. Many entries in my log books were written while I was at the hospital at night awaiting our operative team for a C-section.

I always went to OB the first thing in the morning, and it was my last stop in the afternoon. Why? Very simple. This was our busiest area and the one fraught with the most emergencies. An OB emergency includes cases when the baby is in distress and C-sections are necessary. Things can change almost in the twinkling of an eye. OB might be "quiet" (under control) and in minutes a new arrival could appear with an obstetrical emergency (fetal distress, excess bleeding, shock, eclampsia, malpresentation, and a host of others). Even when I went down at night for a problem on another ward, I would check OB before I left the hospital. The main reason was that I wanted to avoid "surprises". I wanted to know about potential problems, so that I could watch them closely. Earlier in my time at Chimala I would come back and check several times at night — giving the ladies a chance to deliver vaginally. This proved to be fraught with too many problems. Also I was dependent on the midwives and their ongoing assessments. Remember that they had no fetal monitoring system, and babies could get into trouble rather quickly. Consequently, as time went on I tended to do C-sections earlier rather than wait for that 3AM call.

Our labor room had three beds in a room about 10X25 feet. Crowded doesn't begin to describe it. Add in the stifling heat, the nurses and patients, the smells, poor lighting, the various cries; and you may begin to get the picture. I must tell you that our women received nothing for pain. Let me repeat that; NOTHING. As I've stated elsewhere, the women know that having babies is painful; and they expect it. They don't ask for anything for pain. Besides, we didn't have proper pain medicine. Those of you in the USA who've had babies with perhaps an epidural, just think about this. Women in Tanzania are so tough! In the throes of a painful contraction or pushing, they often would just snap their fingers or grit their teeth (of course some occasional yelling and grunting — wouldn't you?)

I keep referring to C-sections. You may be wondering how an ER doctor does C-sections. Of course I knew that in a hospital in Africa, C-sections were the most common surgery, and I'd probably be the only doctor there. Therefore, I had to learn to do them. Why so many C-sections. Simple. So many babies and so little prenatal care. I had done a few sections in Nigeria in the past, having learned from Dr. Farrar. In preparation for moving to Tanzania, I scrubbed in with some of my surgery friends in the USA — reading, assisting in surgery, and making meticulous notes. Ready or not; nervous or not; here I come. I'm not trying to be flippant; I really felt prepared and knew what I was doing.

In the USA the Obstetrical history will include the Gravida, Para, and Abortion status. Gravida stands for the number of pregnancies a woman has had. Para refers to the number of births, and Abortion refers to the number of spontaneous abortions (miscarriages). For example: Gr 2 — P 1 — Ab 0 — this means a woman is in her second pregnancy and has delivered one child and had no abortions. In Tanzania another category is added: Gr — P — Ab — A — The "A" stands for Alive. There are so many babies who die at birth or soon after that this "A" is added. This is just another example of the difference between the Third World and your world. Let me give you just one example. It's regarding a lady I took care of at Chimala. She was Gr 8 — P 7 — Ab 1 — A 2. Let me interpret for you. She had 8 pregnancies, delivered 7, had 1 spontaneous abortion, and now had only 2 alive. One of the children who was alive was the one we had just delivered. Wonderful! Similar situations were not unusual at all.

I performed many more C-sections in my five years at Chimala than all other surgeries put together. I performed some 350 sections in those years. We only did C-sections when it was medically necessary — for the mother or the baby. We didn't do them for "convenience". I did more each succeeding year — depending on whether we had another doctor. Also the reputation of our hospital spread, so that more women came for OB care. As I've stated, this was a mixed blessing. I was quite happy to help more women, but in the meantime yours truly worked harder and harder and lost more sleep. It's a sacrifice I was most grateful to make.

I think we lost two ladies after their C-sections. This was during my first year and before I realized the prevalence of HIV/AIDS. Both these women had the disease and became septic after surgery — (HIV/AIDS renders people so much more susceptible to infection). Sepsis is an overwhelming whole body infection which is often quite resistant to treatment even in otherwise healthy people. Both these ladies died.

I've said that the only thing predictable about OB is its unpredictability. Unless you can accept this, it can be maddening. We might go three days without any C-sections and then have nine in the next three days. My journal records this very scenario one week in June 1995. As you might guess, six of these were at night. This epitomizes OB. Don't forget that I had a hospital full of other patients and various other emergencies during this time. I'm not a martyr or asking for sympathy. It's just what was done. Of course it's hard, but we just accept it.

Let me conclude my OB section with one humorous story — at least I think it's funny. Lou Ann didn't agree. It was your typical hot and steamy evening in OB. We had nursing students from Harding University with us. They were novices and quite excited about the possibility of delivering a baby. As I recall, the Labor Room was full with three ladies in labor. The heat, humidity, stench, and noise were prevalent as usual. In this setting one of the ladies in labor was standing on her bed stark naked while pounding on the wall and crying out, "nimekufa". This means, "I am dying" and is not an unusual outcry during advanced labor. As her labor progressed, she then lay properly on her bed. I was standing to the side observing as the Tanzanian midwife was instructing our students. I could see that delivery was imminent because the membranes were bulging from her vagina. Sometimes the amniotic sac (membranes) don't rupture. When they rupture, the amniotic fluid that surrounds the baby in the uterus is released. Actually it is best to release the fluid — thus giving more room for the baby's head to deliver. In this case the membranes kept coming out of the vagina like one growing balloon. One of our students, Jennifer Johnson, kept getting closer and closer to the bulging membranes, saying, "Wow, look at that." I said nothing but knew what was coming. A moment later — "POW"! You got it; the membranes ruptured — spraying Jennifer and the entire area with fluid. The shriek; the laughter — medicine has to have some levity. Mother and baby did well. [I should tell you that I'd known Jennifer since she was a small child, having grown up in Indianapolis. She's a great sport. I think someone heard her say, "I'll never have children." Let the record show that she now has four children].

MORE "TIDBITS"

*"For every complex question or situation there is a simple solution ……..
neat, plausible, and wrong!"*

– H.L. Mencken

- <u>What are the most difficult things to find in "our Africa?"</u>:

If you've been there, you know the answer. Just think about car travel
in the USA and what you take for granted — good, well marked roads;
regular exits complete with fuel, food, and various amenities; proper sig-
nage; no animals or wreckages on the road; etc. The quick answer is that
we had the antithesis in Africa. First of all fuel stops didn't always mean
that they would actually have fuel. Consequently, we often carried a
"jerry can" with five gallons of diesel. In addition our trusty Land Cruiser
had an extra tank with a range of about 600 miles. It was not unusual for
fuel stations not to have bathrooms. If they did, it was usually a hole in
the floor — dubbed a "squatty potty". We males had the distinct advantage. Often we resorted to "guys on the right" and "ladies on the left", as
we headed to the bushes.

In addition to bathrooms, my list would include running water,
soap, and of course TP (toilet paper). Don't leave home without it! If
you were lucky enough to find some TP, get ready for the strange quality
of the paper. How can I describe it? Hmmm, let me see. If you remember what we used to call 'crape paper', that's basically what it was like —
rough, stretchy, and poorly absorbent (same as we had in language
school). Expectations in bathrooms also include mirrors. I dare you to
find one where we lived. I can't leave off trash cans. About as hard to
find as 'hen's teeth'.

In the USA you can't turn around without having a bathroom and
trash can readily available. I personally think it's rather absurd to have 'no
touch' soap and water dispensers, drying devices, and automatic flushes.
Am I the only one who feels foolish at times — waving my hand in front
of some machine that's not doing anything and wondering if it works?

What about food? In the USA we're used to our usual infinite variety of food and drink choices at an infinite variety of easily accessible locations. Nay, nay at our African stops. Most of the food items available were locally made, so we had to be most careful about food choices — thanks to our overly sensitive stomachs. So guess what; we usually traveled with a goodly supply of food and water.   By the way, do you have any idea what items were ubiquitous? — Coke and Pepsi. Amazing. What about 'fast food'? Certainly not. I'll tell you what we started calling our "drive through" food. Along the mountainous roads near Iringa where the steepness and curves forced our slow pace, venders sold corn ears roasted at the roadside. We often bought these, and the taste was good — a bit tough like what we call "field corn" in Indiana and not "sweet corn."

- <u>What do we have too much of in the USA and not enough of in Africa?:</u>

This is a trick question. The answer is <u>choices</u>. If you've been to the super market lately, you know exactly what I mean — 100 varieties of soft drinks; bread made of every imaginable type of flour; 20 brands of BBQ sauce; 20 kinds of olive oil; 100 kinds of cereal; and on and on it goes. Let me tell you a story about cereal. Once when we were home on leave, Lou Ann went to the market to buy some items. Cereal was on her list, but then she came to the cereal aisle and the myriad of choices. She was so overcome by the volume that she couldn't make a choice and came home without any. True story.

I have to tell you the story of the "fans" also. A few years after moving back to the USA, we had a house built in Indianapolis — our once in a lifetime venture. We worked on our plans extensively and had seemingly an infinite number of choices to make. I'll just share the one about the fans. Like many houses we had some ceiling fans. Isn't a fan a fan? Absolutely not we uninformed found out. We spent an entire morning at the store that installed our fans and lighting fixtures. The number of fan choices was more than unbelievable: size; design; color; light or no light included; if lights were included, there was the number, color, shape of globe; and then the blades — their size, shape, number, angle, color, and "a partridge in a pear tree". I know I've left out several choices. During the process with a 'consultant' I began to feel stupid — no ashamed, as my mind went back to most of the houses in Chimala. If they had electricity at all, there was usually a single cord dangling from the center of the house with a solitary uncovered bulb — usually a 40 watt bulb.

A note here about buying bulbs in Tanzania. They were sold one at a time in the market. There would be a bulb receptacle on the counter so that the bulb could be 'tested' — to make sure it was good. I'm not sure what happened if the electricity was off and there was no generator? Either buy the bulb in good faith or return it later I suppose.

- ## TV and E-Mail: What are these?

When we moved to Chimala, there were no TV stations that reached us. We did have a "TV set", but it was purely to have the luxury of playing video cassettes (remember those?) — for movies, ball games, family events. We often had "Friday night at the movies" — complete with popcorn. What a delight! E-mail was just becoming widespread about this time (1992). When I went to a Christian Men's Retreat in Kenya, there were only two of us that didn't get e-mail. It sounded like it would be a great thing to have. Yes, I felt left out. We did have a radio, but all the local stations were in Swahili. We never were good enough at language to appreciate these stations. What to do? Ours was a short wave radio and could pick up VOA (Voice of America) and BBC (British Broadcasting Corporation). We listened to both; however, we preferred BBC. They had more world news. They made this one mispronunciation that still has us laughing. You may remember the Branch Davidians and the horrible situation in Waco, Texas. We were listening intently as BBC referred to the situation occurring in "Wacko", Texas (humor in the midst of tragedy).

(We were recently in Waco, and I called it "Wacko" throughout our stay).

- "The Keys; The Keys":

Chimala was no different from any other place in that people pilfer and steal. Of course many of our patients and workers had such a paltry amount of money and things. This is no excuse, but it necessitated the proverbial locks. So every door, cabinet, nook and cranny was locked and had a key (yes, an old fashioned key). It drove me crazy until I had that heavy wad of keys with me. Being at the hospital day and night and holidays and weekends, I needed a key for EVERYTHING. Don't tell anyone, but I've been known to break into more than one door or cabinet in my day — usually at night and due to my impatience or because of a faulty lock or key.

- "Racist Dogs"?

Our compound had guards at night that circulated around the perimeter. Their only weapons would be a machete and a club. Some had a dog with them — usually an African Ridgeback. It's a truism that people everywhere are fearful of snarling dogs. Having said this, these dogs uniformly would bark and charge toward unknown people — black visitors but not white visitors. Why? Was it the color, the odor, the familiarity? I don't know the answer. This did present a problem for the missionary children on our compound. Their black friends from across the road in Chimala village were afraid to come and play.

- The Southern Cross:

The Southern Cross is a constellation of stars that's seen in the Southern hemisphere (not visible North of the Equator). We were about 9 degrees South of the Equator in Chimala. It was easily visible from our house over the top of the 3,800 foot mountains that rose immediately behind us. At that time we had no compound lighting; and consequently, there was virtually zero ambient light. This setting rendered the Southern Cross magnificently. Every night when I was called to the hospital, I would pause while gazing on this wonder of God's creation.

- Sounds of Chimala:

I've mentioned the sounds emanating from the OB labor room. Now I'll mention the collage of other sounds that interrupted our nights. I'll start with the sounds of our guards ("watchnight") as they strategically walked quite closely by our bedroom window. Often their dogs would bark incessantly — usually at other dogs, snakes, various animals, and not at intruders. We had a host of household noises — the scurrying of various critters on our walls and floor; rats and bats doing war in the attic; and of course the buzzing of the mosquitos that found a way through the net. I can't leave out the loud music speakers from just across the road at the "maduka" (small shops). These were incessant until around midnight and always played the repetitive style of local rock music. More than once I threatened to take a shot gun and blast away at the speakers (just kidding). A most pleasant sound that was conducive to excellent sleep was the tropical rain on our tin roof. We still miss that. Of course in the midst of a huge tropical downpour, the thundering noise would awaken us. But we didn't mind. I can't leave out the crunching sound from the roadway as someone was walking to my house. Oh no! Being a light sleeper I could hear it right away and knew what they wanted. Moments later I'd hear those telltale words at my window, "Hodi; shida OB" (Hello; problem in OB). And off I'd go. Once in a while we'd hear the distant sound of drums. We never knew the meaning of this. One of the most prevalent and obnoxious sounds emanated from the buses on the roadway — signaling their arrival and departure. Every horn sound and tune devised by man was displayed from the buses. And each driver tried to 'one up' the others with the volume. I'm not exaggerating. Once I said that I've heard every song except "Dixie" from the buses. Wouldn't you believe it; about a week later guess what I heard? Yep. Occasionally when there was a village tragedy I could hear the hubbub of a large crowd at the hospital. This always signaled something bad, so I would get ready to go check it out. Lastly I'll mention that all too frequent doleful wailing from the morgue. It would begin at 6AM and continue for about an hour. In their culture only women did the wailing as they mourned the death of a family member or friend.

- Economy:

During our years in Tanzania the government's minimum wage went up yearly — average of 70% per year. Astonishing! Just imagine if your wages increased like this. Of course all other pricing follows suit, and you're back where you started from. One result is that the Tanzanian shilling is only accepted in Tanzania. Consider the price of postage stamps. The average stamp price increased each year by 100-200%. Compare this to the USA where every few years our stamps increase by 1-2 cents. Just two other examples that help define — "What is Third World?".

- Elections and Voting Day:

In 1995 there was an election for the President of Tanzania. This event had been talked about and greatly anticipated for the two years we had been in Tanzania. This was only the third President that Tanzania had elected since their independence in 1961. A huge time in the country! There is no two party system like the USA. This year there were six candidates.

Chimala had been selected as one of the voting precincts. As voting day approached (always on Sunday), many people streamed into our village from surrounding locales. But then Sunday arrived, and the people all seemed to just be loitering around. What's going on? We found out the ballots had not arrived. What? Something as anticipated and known about for years had a major snafu. We found out that other areas had the same situation. Zanzibar had a "re-vote" for supposed irregularities. So what happened? All the affected areas voted the following Sunday (the ballots had arrived in Chimala). Why had all this happened? Another example of my ongoing question. Such "hiccups" were common and just taken in stride.

A rather humorous aside happened during the Presidential campaign. On of the six candidates and his entourage stopped by Chimala one evening and requested our Guest House for the night. We were glad to comply. Shortly thereafter a messenger came to my house and wanted me to see the candidate regarding a medical situation. I met him in my office at the hospital. He was very kind and quite professional. (No, he didn't win the election). As it turns out, he was on blood pressure and diabetic tablets. He showed me his medicines, and they were OUT OF DATE. This was most paradoxical and also humorous; since the entire country seemed to be acutely aware of not using out of date medicines. I said nothing. After my examination, I gave him some of our IN DATE medicines.

THE DOCTOR BECOMES A PATIENT

*"In the confrontation between the stream and the rock, the stream always wins
….. not through strength, but through persistence."*

[At the outset of this chapter I want to apologize for such a long personal story. However, people seem to get some vicarious enjoyment out of my tale of woe. It also points out some major differences in our health care systems.]

We had just returned from furlough in early January 1996. (By the way, during our break we had the delight of spending Christmas with family for the first time in four years. I also had the honor of performing the wedding ceremony of our daughter, Jennifer, and her fiance', Eric Marquez.). On my first Saturday back in Chimala I had just finished rounds, and some of us guys were having a 'friendly' game of basketball. As I was beginning my usual 'Jordanesque' drive to the hoop and pushing hard off my left foot, I suddenly went down. I knew what was wrong before I hit the concrete. I had ruptured my Achilles tendon. Oh no!! "But I just got back from furlough." "What shall I do?" "Can I get it repaired?"

You never forget such things — the 'snap' followed by searing pain in the heel area. Many years earlier, while playing tennis, I had ruptured my opposite Achilles. That time it was surgically repaired the same day in Indianapolis — even though it was *Labor Day*. But what about here? I'm in Tanzania and know of no orthopedist I want to entrust with my Achilles. "And who's going to cover the hospital; I just returned from furlough." These and more thoughts raced through my mind amidst the pain.

I was helped into my house; and Gary Petty, a visiting medical student from West Virginia, helped ice it and then apply a plaster splint.

What to do? What about a surgical repair? I knew I could just cast it, let it heal 'as is', and perhaps have a delayed surgical repair. Then at some point I remembered the orthopedic surgeon in Nairobi who had operated on one of our missionary's child. He had fractured his femur while bicycle jumping. When John's family returned to the Mission, Dr. Mulimba had sent along good operative notes, post-operative instructions, and a copy of the X-rays showing a very good surgical repair. But was he available? Remember; no phone.

Since it was getting late, we decided to set off on our 'journey of faith' to Dar es Salaam in the early morning. We would try and catch a flight to Nairobi late in the day. Lou Ann had never driven all the rugged five hundred miles from Chimala to Dar es Salaam by herself. In addition she had a disabled, moaning husband in the back of our Toyota Land Cruiser. But like the champ she is, all was accomplished.

I should share something else here. The only significant pain medicine in our entire hospital was one multi-dose vial of injectable Demerol. Orally we had nothing stronger than Ibuprofen. So we set out on our uncertain safari with appropriate syringes and the single vial of Demerol. Before going very far, the all too typical chuck hole 'canyons' that passed as roadway jarred my leg and caused severe muscle spasms. (The largest muscle in the calf is attached to the Achilles tendon.). Lou Ann kept saying, "You've got to take something for pain." Finally I acquiesced. So she gave her very first shot in her hubby's 'bohunkus' in the back of our vehicle somewhere along the Tanzanian roadway.

I have little memory of our journey after that. I'm sure I cannot say the same for Lou Ann. Remember, we had no telephone access and consequently couldn't call to check on flights or make reservations. She drove directly to the airport once we reached Dar. And wouldn't you know it; the last flight to Nairobi had just departed. She made reservations for the first flight the next morning. Dale and Elnora Dennis, our missionary friends in Dar, graciously took over once we arrived at their house. And they had a phone!! Amazingly and thankfully, I was able to reach Dr. Mulimba. He said that he would meet us at Nairobi Hospital the next day. (PTL). *Ajabu sana kabisa* — frankus blackus Swahili version of, "Wow"!

As before, the trip from Dar to Nairobi was quite the blur. I do remember, however, being very impressed with the services at the Nairobi airport, as I was escorted via wheelchair. A missionary picked us up at the airport and took us to the Nairobi Hospital. The receiving area was about as congested as you would imagine in this location. And Murphy's Law was still in effect. True to form as with doctors anywhere in the world, Dr. Mulimba had some emergency cases ahead of me. The hours snailed by as I sat in pain and increasing hunger. I didn't want food on my stomach that might cause a delay in surgery. It had already been more than two days since the injury. What was Lou Ann doing during this time? I have no idea. Pain has a way of squeezing your world into a very small, self-focused entity.

After several hours, I was taken to my room and continued waiting for surgery. As I remember, it was about an eight hour wait. The room was clean yet Spartan, and it was private! The nurses reminded me of the USA from the 1950's, being all prim and proper and starchy white, with their nurse caps properly worn. At some point a young Indian lady, dressed in her traditional sari, arrived and politely introduced herself as the anesthesiologist. She went on to say that general anesthesia would be needed. (In case you don't know, this type anesthesia not only entails being asleep but also might require being paralyzed and put on a ventilator.). I consider this type anesthesia "overkill" for my type procedure. The risk of anesthesia would be much greater than the risk of surgery. At that point I told her I wanted it done under spinal anesthesia. She said, *"We don't have spinal pontocaine at night. The pharmacy is closed."* (Pontocaine is one of the chemicals that anesthetizes the nerves when placed in the spinal canal.). I promptly responded, *"Yes you have some."* While telling her this, I was simultaneously reaching in my shirt pocket and pulling out a vial of pontocaine — in addition to a spinal needle.

This is indeed the exact way it happened. Lou Ann is my witness. Such a story as this needs absolutely no embellishment.

I should back up one step. I neglected to tell you that in our hasty preparation for the trip from Chimala to Nairobi, I had gathered various supplies. Why? In my experience in Africa I had learned that quite often patients and families are sent to find their own supplies and medicines. And I believe in preparation! Was I ready or what?!

She really did an excellent job in administering my spinal. Without being facetious I can tell you that I was the PERFECT patient. Yes; I was. You see — I have administered many spinals to patients, and perhaps the most important thing is to have a cooperative patient who will be absolutely still. This assists the doctor in introducing the needle into the spinal canal, where the medicine is placed. I held absolutely still in the position she wanted.

After placing the medicine in the canal, she told me to keep sitting. I should say here that after I performed spinals, I assisted the patient in lying down while keeping the head and shoulders a bit elevated. This is so that the medicine will not rise too high in the canal and interfere with breathing. In my particular situation as a patient, however; things were a bit different. I had not had anything by mouth in ten hours and consequently was probably a bit dehydrated. This factor, plus the effect of the spinal on the nerves, caused a significant drop in my blood pressure. After about fifteen seconds, that horrible queasy, weak, nauseated, fainty feeling was rapidly coming over me. As I began to try and lie down, she said, *"Oh, don't do that."* I continued to lie back while saying to her, *"If I don't lie down now, I'm going to faint."* — I didn't faint.

After the spinal had taken full effect, Dr. Mulimba began taking off the original plaster splint that had been put on at Chimala. I should interject here that he had not yet examined my leg. His very words upon removing the last of the splint and dressings were, *"It's not ruptured."* Just as quickly and undauntedly I replied, *"Look again."* Upon further examination he said, *"Oh yes, the muscle has retracted up the leg."* After this, the surgery went uneventfully. I should say here that Dr. Mulimba did a very good repair that has stood the test of time.

Lou Ann and I went to the Church of Christ Guest House in Nairobi the next day and spent one night. All was going alright — well, except for one thing. I had an absolutely horrible post-spinal headache. This doesn't mean anything was done wrong. It's an expected side effect in a certain number of cases. I should explain about "spinal headaches". The needle that introduces the anesthetic penetrates what is called the dura and enters the spinal canal in the mid lower back area. Sometimes the hole that is left by the twenty-one gauge needle doesn't seal completely. This results in leakage of spinal fluid into the surrounding soft tissues. The effect on the brain as the fluid is lost is one terrific headache. Because of the effect of gravity, the headache is much, much more severe in the upright position. So the treatment is to lie down, drink plenty of fluids, take something for the headache, and wait. Don't worry; the hole eventually closes and the leakage stops. But it may take several days. There is a treatment to stop the leakage sooner called a "blood patch". I won't go into that, for I never even considered letting the doctors do the procedure.

Don't ask me why but the very next day we flew back to Tanzania. This was a stupid move then and in retrospect still looms up there in my personal annals of stupid decisions. I've already told you about my gosh awful, horrendous headache. To elucidate further, every time I sat up or stood up I was soon hit with a worsening headache. This was accompanied by horrible waves of nausea. With this lovely picture in mind as I elucidate further, you'll agree with my stupidity.

Off we now went to the Nairobi airport with my headache in full force, the nausea, and oh yes; don't forget I was on crutches and not quite two days post-op. Any leg pain had easily been supplanted by the spinal headache. To make matters worse, the air conditioner in our car was not working. The heat of the day and the stench of diesel fumes made the situation almost unbearable. *"How can I do this!?"*

Somehow we managed to check in at the airport and went to the gate area to await our flight. My misery kept increasing. I was almost at my wits' end. (Even now I can hardly believe what I did next, but here goes. Truth is stranger than fiction.). I said, *"Lou Ann, I can't take this anymore."* I took the vial of Demerol, a syringe and needle, and crutched to the men's restroom. I awkwardly went into a stall, closed the door, loaded the syringe with 75mg of Demerol, exposed the necessary anatomy, and gave myself a shot in ye ol' bohunkus. Of course I was trying to be quite secretive about the whole ordeal. The entire process would be too ludicrous and far fetched to explain. If I'd been caught, I would probably still be in a Nairobi jail. And what I didn't know at the time was that since I was taking so long, Lou Ann had sent someone in to check on me. He came back and told her that someone was in the stall. Fortunately that must have been all he saw.

I put the incriminating evidence away, crutched back to the waiting area, and then lay flat on the floor with the curious crowds milling by. I couldn't have cared less. Finally some relief!

At this point I definitely failed one of our ongoing dictums. That being, *"If it's funny later, then it's funny now."* For some reason I could find no humor while lying on the floor of the busy Nairobi airport, in pain, and having just "shot up" in the men's bathroom.

We did have the foresight to stay in Dar es Salaam for a couple of days. One problem, however, and once again affirming Murphy's Law — the long awaited air conditioning in the hotel did not work Oh well;

"TIA" (This is Africa"). The spinal headache lasted about five days and was down to a dull roar as we headed back to Chimala.

I'll conclude this all too lengthy personal saga with one lasting memory from the recovery stage of my surgery. Crutching from my house to the hospital and making rounds really posed no particular problems. What I do remember is doing surgery (mostly Caesarean sections) while standing on one leg and using my casted leg for balance. C-sections are fraught with generous amounts of blood and amniotic fluid. Consequently, I carefully protected my plaster cast with plastic garbage bags; so as not to…….. well, use your imagination.

FOURTEEN OFFICES & FOUR HOURS LATER

"The difficulties of living in a Third World country have a unique way of draining energy and leaving one feeling overwhelmed by the needs of others."

— Steve Sherman

[This came directly from my Newsletter of May 1993]

Does the title sound like a new book on the best seller list? Well, you're right; it's not. This represented an ordeal, a trial of patience, a gauntlet, and a perfect example of the uncertainty and inefficiency that we affectionately call "TIA" (This is Africa). Lou Ann and Janice had the honor of this particular experience. It all started at the Government Central Medical Stores in Dar es Salaam on a Monday morning. We had decided to divide and conquer. I was elsewhere running about the maze of Dar looking for some X-ray film (another story). They were at the Stores to try and obtain some pethidine (Demerol — a narcotic pain killer for our patients with burns, fractures, post-operative, etc.). This particular location in Dar is the only place in Tanzania that pethidine could be obtained.

Lest I bore you I will quickly run through the fourteen hoops they had to — OOPS! — I mean offices they had to pass through. Each stop meant waiting, waiting — often to see someone who was not doing anything else and seemed to get some pleasure from the 'power' to make you wait. Patience remember — patience. To show anger or irritation is a guaranteed longer wait or even failure to progress to the next office. In other words; they've got you! You must play by their rules — "When in Rome, do ...." So each stop gave Lou Ann and Janice no guarantee or assurance that they would succeed in their quest. As the hours and offices ticked by, would they make it? Is it really possible? No, probably not. We didn't succeed the last time we tried; why this time? Yet with triumph at successive offices they could not help but have just a twinge of confidence creep in. Can we really make it?

Writer's cramp set in due to a multitude of forms to be filled out in triplicate or more. But Lou Ann and Janice — troopers that they are — persisted in this endurance contest. From the <u>GATE PASS</u> office, then to <u>REQUISITION</u>

their REQUISITION PAPERS, then to the ASSISTANT MANAGER, then to the "BIG MAN", then back to the ASSISTANT MANAGER, back to the "BIG MAN", back to the GATE OFFICE, again to the "BIG MAN", to the GATE OFFICE once more, and again to the REQUISITION OFFICE. (Hey, I'm not making this up!). WHEW! Now to the BILL OFFICE. The home stretch; next to the PAY OFFICE and the finish line. (Does this come to fourteen?). Surely if they take our money we have it made.

I had arrived on the scene during their second stop at the Requisition Office. Lou Ann showed some signs of being frazzled at the edges but was still hanging in there. So we all marched to the Pay Office together. It was now 1:30PM and orders are not taken after 2PM. So near the end. Alas, the office was closed! No one knew where the pay officer was. Were we at a dead end? After completing eleven successful stops were we now stymied? I turned my back, and in the meantime Lou Ann had disappeared with a lady. When I found her thirty minutes later, she had paid someone else (Ajabu! — Swahili for "amazing or wonder"). The lady had been our good Samaritan and gone out of her way to help. Thank you. Lou Ann had gone through steps twelve and thirteen and was at the LAST STOP — the pick up station. She had witnessed a near fight as another man was upset about his order; but not being deterred, she stood her ground. The finish line was in sight. She completed the last '99' signatures and behold, they handed her two small boxes containing 200 vials of pethidine. SUCCESS! Oh Frank of little faith. I had said, "No way." And in only four hours. Who said the system doesn't work?

An exaggeration? No. This is but one example of what must be done to get something accomplished. No phones or inter-office communication or computers in this largest medical storehouse in Tanzania. The epitome of the Third World. The alternative for us would have been to do without. It was well worth the time and frustration.

A SCREAM IN THE NIGHT

"God never brings a hindrance into our lives that He does not intend to be used to open another door that would not have opened otherwise."

– Jamie Buckingham

It was a typical night during rainy season. The heavy rain drops were banging loudly on our tin roof. Loud intermittent percussions of thunder interjected themselves. However, it wasn't these expected and appreciated sounds that awoke us. At about 3AM Lou Ann and I were awakened by the anguished, loud cries of a woman in distress. What in the world is going on? We lay there listening while trying to figure out what was going on and if we should do anything. The cries were intermittent but incessant as they penetrated the sounds of the storm. Could this be a woman wailing at the morgue, which was a scant one hundred yards from our house? No, because wailing didn't begin until about dawn. It was pitch black. The agonizing crying/screaming/wailing was unrelenting. It kept vacillating as the storm sounds waxed and waned. After about thirty minutes of the haunting sound, we decided it just couldn't be a person. But what was it? We found out in the morning upon going to the hospital. A dog had fallen into the burn pit and couldn't get out.

What made this situation even more strange — bizarre in fact — was what Lou Ann found out when she went into the Women's Ward. She was just passing through with her usual "habari asubuhi" (good morning) and asked the head nurse how things were. The nurse said, "Oh mama, everyone is very tired today." Of course Lou Ann asked why? The nurse told Lou Ann how a woman had died during the night and had been taken to the morgue (which was adjacent to the ward). Then it started. The women on the ward began hearing the same strange crying that we had heard. As it went on and on, they just knew that the woman in the morgue was alive and needed help. Some thought her spirit was crying out (one of their animistic beliefs). Lou Ann couldn't convince them otherwise. At any rate the situation had been so unsettling that most had not slept, which of course explained their fatigue.

SOURCES OF STRENGTH

"To go the distance in Missionary Medicine we need to be compelled by a vision, urgent in our response to world healthcare needs, knowledgeable about valleys and detours in the journey, and encouraged by the certainty of God's ultimate victory."
—Evvy Campbell

"When the going gets tough; the tough get going." I don't know the origin of this 'truism', but I completely agree. But it's what God puts inside you and me that keeps us going when things are especially tough and with no end in sight. (Having said this; I know that we all have our limits. There's no shame in this.). I can only speak personally in this regard.

God grants each of us with an inherent degree of toughness — for lack of a better term. We want to finish what we start. We don't want to be called quitters, whether this is on the high school football team or in a job that's more demanding than we expected. The proper, right, good thing to do is to complete our task. But why? Is it personal dedication in order to fulfill a responsibility, the expectation of others, or just not wanting to lose 'face'? The answer is "Yes" — all the above and more. I faced this need for mental toughness and perseverance especially after our first three years in the field. Over our years at Chimala the number of patients kept increasing. Consequently, as it got busier obviously our workload increased. We didn't turn patients away; we wanted to care for the sick and injured. But there are limits. As a physician, I had no comparable doctor staff to share my level of responsibility. Bottom line: the difficult work and decisions were mine and mine alone. (Pediatrics was an exception as I'll explain). On and on and on it went — without a break. My only break would come when I was physically away from the compound.

The analogy I use here is the example of taking care of a lion cub from birth — you're bigger and stronger than it is. It keeps growing and growing until one day it's bigger and stronger and can devour its master. The hospital seemed to be headed in this direction. Also at this point I always think of what Janice says. She reminds me that when I was recruiting her I said, *"The hospital is manageable."* She never let me forget what I'd said.

But what were my sources of strength? I've already mentioned our inherent God given strength. My earnest prayers were offered up regularly to grant me even more strength and perseverance. My wife, Lou Ann, was a constant source of strength. She was always at my side, helping both physically and psychologically. She will tell you that her experiences at Chimala were the highlight of her life of service. She dearly loved the work, the time, the life, the people, and the service she rendered there. This love was apparent to all. She felt more needed and rewarded than at any other time of her life. Her enthusiasm, positive attitude, and encouragement helped keep me going. Of course I loved what I was doing also, but at times it was just "too much" — like too much chocolate cake, too many ball games, too much of anything you like. I talk about this more in another section — on "The Big B.O." (Burn Out)

I'm always 'big' on quotes; they help give me strength, perspective, and a positive attitude. I had several posted on the wall of my office at the hospital that I read every single day. I've included these and many others in the book.

I'll take an aside and tell you two incidences of how Lou Ann was involved in a medical way. You must remember that even though by now she'd been married to a doctor for 30 years, she had no medical training or experience. One night about 9PM I was called to "Minor Theatre" for a trauma case. You absolutely NEVER knew what to expect when you got these calls. Well this evening it turned out to be a man who'd had a chain saw 'kick back' and hit him square in the face. It struck him almost "dead center", cutting him from forehead to chin. His nose was splayed open, as was his upper and lower lips — exposing his inner nose and his teeth and gums. Quite a hideous, bloody sight! Being an ER doc, this type trauma was right up my alley. Even though it looked serious, we call this minor trauma. He was fully awake and alert and wanting to be fixed.

I had the proper instruments and suture needed, the local anesthetic, and surgical soap needed to do the repair. Two problems: I had no assistant and the power was off. No problem. Lou Ann volunteered to be my assistant. I had my trusty AA Mini-Maglite so that she could illuminate the surgical field. First I had to inject the wound with zylocaine in order to numb it and then clean it extremely well. The most important part of wound care is to clean the wound, removing any dirt, foreign material, or dead tissue. And yes, river water is just fine. You see; the water from our faucets was directly from the river. It's the washing or irrigation of the wound that's the most important. Besides, the most common bacteria in river water (Escherichia coli) is not what causes wound infections.

Now I proceeded to close the jagged wound margins from forehead to chin. As I was trying to do a meticulous, proper cosmetic closure, the small circle of light kept disappearing from my surgical field. I'd say, "Lou Ann, hold the light steady; I can't see what I'm doing." Her response was, "Well, if you want to know the truth, when I hold the light in the field, I have to look closely; and this makes me feel like I'm going to faint." In her defense, the wound was rather hideous. Also the heat and subsequent sweat running down our faces, along with the smell of blood, plus the other noxious odors in Minor Theatre didn't help matters any.

I did finish the repair successfully and sent him off to the ward. And yes, Lou Ann, the trooper that she is, made it to the end. The wound healed well and looked quite good, if I do say so myself. And Lou Ann proved to be a stalwart assistant many other times.

I would be negligent if I didn't mention the strength and support of Janice Bingham. Janice is a Nurse Practitioner who made the journey with us from beginning to end. I first met Janice in 1981 when she was serving as a Nurse at Nigerian Christian Hospital. At that time I was a rank beginner in tropical medicine, not to mention the vagaries of third world medicine. I recognized then that Janice was not only very intelligent, but that she had tremendous clinical skills and savvy — a valuable asset in the field of medicine. Later she got her Pediatric Nurse Practitioner's degree. I didn't have to think long when I was trying to recruit a Nurse to go to Tanzania with Lou Ann and me. Fortunately, she accepted.

Janice was indefatigable. She could run a Pediatric ward of seventy-five sick, crying kids single-handedly, with only a modicum of help from me. Amazing! She accomplished all this without complaining and always with compassion and the readiness to take care of the next "low sick"child ("low sick" according to Janice is a Jacks Creek, Tennessee term for someone who is quite ill.). Besides her work habits, her personality and Christian manner also served as fine examples that encouraged me. I think it's now obvious why Janice helped give me strength to continue my work.

My family gave us full support for what Lou Ann and I were doing. This included our children (Melanie, Jeffrey, and Jennifer), our parents, in-laws, and others. We had many church friends and other contacts that supported us emotionally, monetarily, spiritually, and in many other ways. By taking care of matters "back home", any possible concerns we had there were taken away.

(By the way, we were blessed with Jeffrey and Jennifer visiting us. And oh yes, Jennifer's fiance', Eric Marquez, came with them. Meeting your future son-in-law for the first time at the Dar es Salaam airport is rather........ shall I say uncomfortable and unusual. Everything worked out great.)

HIV / AIDS

"God does not hold us responsible for success. He holds us responsible for obedi-ence. He does not demand that we accomplish great things, but that we attempt them."

–David Augsburger

I begin this chapter on HIV/AIDS with the only Newsletter article that I wrote solely on this serious topic during our five years in Chimala.

AIDS AT CHIMALA (March 8, 1996)

Other than briefly mentioning AIDS in perhaps two previous Newsletters, we have stayed away from this subject. Yet it is what we are asked about the most. Why have we not written about it? It's probably a combination of con-cerns ranging from incredulity to misunderstandings. I want to address some of these issues so as to inform you as well as to challenge you.

PLEASE REMEMBER

As I have stated before, HIV/ AIDS at Chimala and in East Africa is a <u>*heterosexual disease.*</u> *I must always say this at the outset because most of you in the USA think that AIDS is basically a homosexual disease. (This is true in the USA; however, heterosexual transmission of HIV/AIDS is increasing in the USA).*

FACTS AND FIGURES

Most of you know that East Africa is one of the areas in the world that had the earliest and has the heaviest incidence of AIDS. Why? There are several theories regarding this on which I won't elucidate now. Perhaps our most asked question is, "What is your incidence of AIDS at Chimala?" The best answer I *can give you comes from two sets of statistics we have gathered. Once per year a government sponsored study is done on 200 pregnant mothers attending our Maternal Clinic. The age range is from mid-teens to about 40. These women are not clinically sick — just coming for a routine OB visit. The percentage that test positive for HIV at Chimala is 16-17%. (Some of the highest figures from other similar clinics in Tanzania are in the range of 39% — astounding!) Our second figure comes from the routine HIV testing of all potential blood donors. These are supposedly healthy relatives or friends of patients needing blood (the age range of donors generally runs between the late teens to the 50's). The percent of potential blood donors who test positive for HIV is 17%. Because of these two similar percentages, we can assume that for the age group mentioned, 17% of the <u>community is infected with the AIDS virus.</u> They aren't ill with clinical AIDS (yet) but would be called HIV positive. (Depending on where you are in the USA a similar study group may be lower than 1%). There is simply no way to sufficiently describe our situation. Devastating, overwhelming, epidemic, rampant, crisis, scourge, cataclysmic — these words only begin to tell the story. On a singular positive note — the percent of positives from blood donors decreased in 1995. Time will tell.*

We do HIV testing on out-patients and in-patients who are ill and in whom clinical AIDS is a possibility. Of all such patients tested two-thirds are found to have clinical AIDS. Staggering! Another figure you should find interesting is that of the new cases of AIDS we identify, <u>the number of men and women are essentially equal.</u> This is a predictable finding where AIDS is heterosexually transferred and where homosexuality is taboo.

TRANSMISSION OF AIDS

Similar to the USA I would have to say that many people here are sexually promiscuous (more prevalent in some tribes than others). Also this is a very male dominant culture. The women are not all innocent; but much of the AIDS here is blamed on the men bringing it home. Many men work far from their homes for extended periods of time and unfortunately visit prostitutes. If this is the situation, then the women become the innocent victims. The trans-

mission of the AIDS virus to the unborn child from HIV positive mothers runs somewhere between 30% and 50%. These children are the <u>very epitome of innocent victims</u>. Breast milk can also transfer the virus to the child (figures regarding the virus transfer usually run between 10-20%). Hold back the breast milk you say. Then the child would likely die of starvation — most of our patients do not have cows nor the money to buy milk substitutes. Besides, to not breast feed a child in this culture is just not accepted.

Transmission is also enhanced here by much ignorance and denial. Many have a laissez-faire attitude. Others go to the extent of thinking that people get AIDS like you get pneumonia or malaria (fatalistic concept). DON'T WORRY: AIDS is not spread by mosquitoes. This can easily be explained away by the fact that AIDS is not equal in all age groups (not in small children for example). Whereas malaria, which is caused by mosquitoes, is pretty much equal across all age groups. If AIDS were spread by mosquitoes, then there would be an equal spectrum of the disease across all age groups. This is not the case.

What more vile disease could some diabolical demonic being come up with than a disease like AIDS. There has never been a disease like it — a disease in which your body barely even recognizes the virus as a foreign agent; the virus can become part of your own cell reproduction process; the virus can essentially "go into hiding" for extended periods; your disease fighting cells (your immune system) are slowly but persistently depleted; the infection by the virus proceeds clinical illness (symptoms) sometimes by many years — thus making infecting someone else much more likely; the virus seems capable of frequent mutations; the virus has proven itself quite resistant to treatment. Where is the answer? God gave men the ability to find answers, and I feel confident one will come. But the simplest and best answer to eradicate the disease is through the practice of God's laws of sexuality.

FROM ONE DOCTOR "IN THE TRENCHES"

Overwhelmed? Feelings of futility? Sadness? Pity? Such a waste of the young? Concern for personal contamination? Besieged by ethical dilemmas? Yes, yes, and more. This very day I diagnosed four new cases of AIDS in the hospital — all so sick. (669 new in-patient cases in 1995, plus the 199 HIV positive blood donors). AIDS is the great masquerader — it can present as almost any other disease. If a patient at Chimala is quite sick or has some finding we don't understand, it becomes our automatic response to first test for AIDS. We have no definitive AIDS medicines to offer! Too expensive. We do have AIDS counselors and offer limited home care nursing. Our capabilities for helping these patients fit into the "band-aid on the cancer" mode of treatment. With our limited medicines and resources who gets what treatment? Who gets admitted and for how long? Do you operate? DECISIONS!? What would Jesus do?

I'll let some of my Log Book notes speak of my feelings regarding HIV/AIDS at that time.

Entry dated April 4, 1997:

"Defeated; futility; hopeless; helpless; impotent; might as well walk away. What am I describing?

Eight cases on Female Ward rounds today:

1. *25 year old with constant convulsions*
2. *23 year old with large pelvic abscess*
3. *24 year old very thin, very short of breath; pneumonia*
4. *23 year old very weak and unexplained high fever*
5. *19 year old very thin with severe diarrhea*
6. *22 year old with encephalopathy, decreased consciousness*
7. *23 year old with empyema (pus in the chest usually from severe pneumonia)*
8. *25 year old very thin, pneumonia, TB*

All these ladies have advanced end-stage clinical AIDS. See what I mean!"

You can see that the age group most affected by this horrible disease is the young adults. It takes away the mothers and fathers, the workers, the teachers, the future leaders, etc. The family as well as the social, financial, educational, and most other areas in the community are direly affected.

Another Log Book entry:

"I started rounds on male ward today with fourteen known cases of AIDS (14 out of 35 total patients). By the end of rounds there were three more new admissions that were very likely to be AIDS cases (they turned out to be positive),"

Now you can begin to identify with my feelings. You see; we had no anti-viral medicines for HIV. NONE! In my 5 years at Chimala I never saw even one AZT tablet (Zidovudine). AZT was the going treatment at that time. (Later this changed drastically and for the patients' benefit.). In my Newsletter article I referred to AIDS presenting in many different ways. This is because the virus takes away our best way to combat infections and tumors — our own God-given immune system. Once that is depleted, our bodies are open to virtually everything. This is why I call HIV/AIDS the "perfect killing machine". It's not the virus itself that attacks us; it's what the virus does to our immune system. The door is opened to any and all opportunistic organisms or agents. In explaining the virus I've used the "Trojan Horse analogy" as follows: The virus seems to pose no threat as it enters the body. But then it basically "fools the body," as it gets inside the cells and attacks from within by destroying the immune system.

I kept a list of the ways AIDS presented at Chimala. As I've stated, anyone who was quite ill or had something unexplainable presumably had AIDS until proven otherwise. With this in mind they would be tested. I kept a list of the myriad ways AIDS presented while I was at Chimala:

- Those most obvious were the people who were wasted — extreme weight loss, chronic diarrhea, etc.
- Any person with TB
- Failure to thrive [children who fail to grow and gain weight]
- Kaposi's sarcoma [a cancerous condition usually on the skin or mucous membranes in the mouth]
- Herpes zoster ["shingles"]. Of all the zoster cases we saw only 2 were not also HIV [+]
- Cardiomyopathy with heart failure [enlarged heart with subsequent failure]
- Any severe abscess or skin infection
- Acute polyarthritis [diffuse joint inflammation]
- Nephrotic syndrome [kidney failure with severe whole body edema (swelling), etc.]
- Anyone with severe post-operative infections
- Primary peritonitis [infection in the peritoneal cavity (abdomen) in the absence of appendicitis, etc.]
- Unexplained coma
- Unexplained confusion or psychosis
- Unexplained seizures
- Presenting as a CVA [Cerebrovascular accident — "stroke"]
- Peripheral neuropathy [unexplained numbness, weakness, paralysis, etc.]
- Jaundice [jaundice is a yellow color to the eyes and skin from liver or gall bladder disease]
- Severe anemia [Low red blood cell count not explainable except by the probable affect of HIV on the bone marrow, which makes red blood cells]

- Premature labor
- Spontaneous abortion
- Near full term intrauterine fetal death
- Primary amenorrhea [young women who never have menstrual periods]
- PID [Pelvic Inflammatory Disease] and tubo-ovarian abscesses
- Thrombophlebitis
- Bleeding disorders [presenting as bleeding gums, continuous nose bleeds, etc.]
- Unexplained shock [extremely low blood pressure]
- Continuous vomiting
- Hoarseness
- Ascites [build up of fluid within the abdominal cavity]
- Pleural effusion [fluid build-up within the chest cavity]
- Continuous hiccups
- Underweight children
- Enlarged lymph nodes
- Yeast infections [monilia]
- Aseptic meningitis [meningitis that is not bacterial — probably caused by HIV itself]
- FUO [Fever of Unknown Origen]
- Pneumonia

From this list you can see what I mean — why we ordered so many HIV tests. It was so sad but true.

I have given many talks on HIV/AIDS, and it's a nebulous honor to be considered an expert in this area. This remains such an atrocious, hideous, horrible, devastating illness in developing country settings. Why, you may ask? Delayed detection due to denial, lack of knowledge, stigma, fear, finances, sexual mores and promiscuity. Then once detected there remains the matter of being absolutely compliant in taking the anti-viral medicines. This again gets into understanding and stigma; also problematic are travel, money, prompt medical care for intervening problems, time involved, etc. Beginning around 2005 in Tanzania the testing, counseling, and medicine are FREE! (Thanks to the Tanzanian and USA governments and the Gates Foundation). Sounds great, doesn't it? Yes, it is; but the downside once again is the compliance rate. So much remains to be done.

I know this chapter is quite 'dark'. That's because of the scourge of this disease. I really can't describe in words my feelings of sadness and futility as I made rounds and saw patient after patient in a helpless and hopeless condition. Many of these patients have been abandoned by their families.

I've given a number of talks on HIV/AIDS in the USA. It's such a devastating and somber area to talk about; how can you possibly begin a presentation? Oftentimes when you give a talk, you start with a joke or a related lighthearted story. Both of these seem inappropriate when approaching this topic. However, I did come up with an introduction that seemed to garner interest while depicting the overall lack of understanding about the disease. I would start a lecture with these real questions I received at the end of a talk on HIV/AIDS in a secondary school in Africa.

My all time favorite question: (I'm not making this up).

"Can you get AIDS by eating the meat of a goat that ate the grass on the grave of someone who died of AIDS?"

Remember, these questions came after a one hour lecture in which I told in simple language what HIV/AIDS is, what causes it, how you get it, how you <u>don't</u> get it, the symptoms and signs, and so forth. These are some other questions I received that day:

- *"What causes HIV/AIDS?"*
- *"How does HIV get into your body?"*

- *"Does blood cause AIDS"?*
- *"How can you know if you have AIDS?"*
- *"Can you get AIDS by touching someone with AIDS"?*
- *"What causes STD's?"*
- *"Can we know the first person to have AIDS in the world?"*

I covered all these areas in my talk. However, I'll give these students an "out." It's possible that my English was not well understood by these African High School students.

THE VICTIM BECOMES THE SAVIOR

*"Peace is not the absence of trouble, trials, and torment; but calm
in the midst of them."*

— Don Meyer

Most of you know the story from the Bible called "The Good
Samaritan." Well, this story goes it one better.

It was a typical Tuesday as Lou Ann was making her weekly shopping run to Mbeya about an hour's drive away. Mbeya was our closest
city — where we received our mail and did any 'major' shopping (actually it was quite limited.). It was also our closest phone connection and
where we attempted to make or receive calls from the United States once
a month.

Usually Lou Ann made her market journey with either Ernest or
John — Tanzanian men who worked for us. But on this particular day
some of the other missionaries also went along to take care of some business. She let them out of the Land Cruiser to visit various offices as she
went shopping in the market — gathering foodstuffs, medicines, etc. At
one point as she was driving along, she saw some commotion up ahead.
Someone along the roadway got her attention and said, *"Mama, someone
has robbed your husband!"* The assumption had been made that Bill was
her husband — after all Bill was white and about the right age. (I was
back at the hospital as usual. During our five years in Chimala I may
have gone with Lou Ann once on her shopping day). At any rate Lou
Ann knew it was Bill he was talking about. As she was assessing the situation, she spotted a crowd on an adjacent street. Among the crowd she
could see Bill's hat bobbing up and down. Bill could be spotted easily as
he ran along, for he was taller and of course the only white man in the
crowd. He did indeed seem to be chasing someone. Being on the adjacent street, Lou Ann drove along trying to keep up with Bill and the

crowd as best possible. After not too long a time, she heard gun shots. She drove as close as possible to the scene at hand. What she then saw was Bill standing by a bleeding man lying on the sidewalk — apparently having been shot.

I should interject here that there had been a rash of robberies in Mbeya around this time. Typically the thieves would plan a distraction; and while you were unaware, a man would quickly snatch your pouch, pack, or whatever. As the thief ran away, he would toss it to someone else. Then they would run in opposite directions — taking a circuitous course in and out of buildings and alleys. In Bill's case he happened to have his pouch in his hand. It was an easy heist for the thief (a lesson for all of us travelers, especially in crowded areas). It contained his passport, money, and other papers.

When a robber was caught, he was frequently killed on the spot in a mob-like action. They were usually beaten or stoned and then burned alive. Someone would put old tires over the person, douse them with kerosene, and ignite a fire. Horrible. A memorable line in the English version of the local Mbeya newspaper about this time was as follows: _"It is illegal to barbeque thieves, whether guilty or innocent."_ I'm not making this up. It was not unusual to have thieves beaten to death, stoned, or incinerated. I saw this several times in our small Chimala village. Usually there would be no legal action against anyone in the crowd. We were told more than once by Tanzanians, _"If someone robs you, just yell "mwizi"; and we will kill them."_ (mwizi means thief.)

The locals had gathered around quickly and had already doused the thief with kerosene. The policeman who had shot him was standing idly by. This is when the 'victim became the savior'. Bill quickly intervened, putting himself between the injured man and the crowd, just as they were about to light the kerosene. After considerable palaver, which caused the scene to escalate, the policeman intervened. Since it was "illegal" to burn thieves; and the situation was escalating by the minute, the policeman probably thought twice about allowing the thief to be killed. What to do?

Since Lou Ann's car was close by, he summoned her to bring it closer. At this point the wounded thief was thrown into the back of our Land Cruiser — still bleeding from the gunshot wound to his hip. Several policemen piled in after him. So off Lou Ann drove to the police station with Bill, thief, and policemen. Lou Ann told me that as she looked in the rear view mirror, she occasionally saw the policemen hit the thief with the butt of their rifles. The thief was dragged into the police station and thrown against the wall as Bill and the policeman made their reports. The thief was surrounded by other police personnel who would occasionally take the liberty of kicking him.

We don't know what eventually happened to the thief. As to Bill's pouch, luckily someone found it not long after. Only the money had been taken, and his passport was still there. This saved the hassle of going five hundred miles to the American Embassy in Dar es Salaam to obtain another passport.

Indeed, "THE VICTIM HAD BECOME THE SAVIOR"

"WHITE MEN ARE WEAK"

"All that is required to maintain incessant, invincible confidence is a willingness to focus on the many things we have in common rather than the few things that make us different."

Before I lunge into a section with such a title, I should hasten to explain that any racial overtones or undertones are purely in the mind of the reader — not this writer. It is written out of a love I have for Africans. True friends can laugh at each other without giving it any more thought, and such is the case here. This love began in 1977 on a trip to Nigeria with a beloved man I call the "Father of Medical Missions" in our church, my mentor, Dr. Henry Farrar. I always called him Henry even though he had about a decade on me. He met an untimely death in 2010. Such a fine, humble, Christian man cannot be duplicated — only emulated. He lived entirely to serve others. And yet, what a character! Everyone who knew Henry has a "Dr. Farrar story".

By comparing some of the amazing qualities of the Africans, I fabricated a list that they might make up about us white Americans. They are the antithesis of African traits; thus my title, "White Men Are Weak". Some of the machinations we missionaries go through must totally confound the African (most of the missionaries I've worked with have been Caucasian). What most of us generically go through to 'not get sick' or to protect ourselves is usually seen as a sign of weakness by the African — not to mention often unnecessary. Every culture has its own social behavior — habits and actions that are deemed acceptable or unacceptable, rude or crude. As missionaries, foreigners, "aliens", we always tried to be sensitive to these social behaviors. But alas, in times of distraction or haste, I confess that I often forgot. Being most magnanimous, however, our African friends were quick to overlook our cultural snafus. On the other hand, I don't think the Africans realized they had habits that were annoying, even obnoxious to us at times. Would you think about your habits if a foreigner came to work with you in your country? No.

Like most people, you would expect them to adapt to you and not vice versa.

I'll start with my list of "weaknesses" I heard or inferred from my Tanzanian friends. By the way, we were generally referred to as "wazungu" (white persons). I've mentioned that the term *wazungu* in Swahili carries the concept of "one who is busily running around to and fro all the time." I think this is rather apropos, don't you? It surely fits me.

So, why are we considered weak?

- Our hair is weak because it's thin and straight
- Our hair is weak because it's 'slick' — this is why we can't carry loads on our heads
- Our eyes are weak — just look at all the glasses and sunglasses we wear, and we have to use a flashlight at night.
- Our weakness is manifested because we don't have a strong body odor. "Besides, strong body odor keeps the mosquitoes away. That's why the wazungu have so much trouble with malaria."
- Our teeth are weak because we always have to have our meat tender, and we can't chew up chicken bones. Also we can't open a coke bottle using our teeth.
- Our feet are weak because we always have to wear shoes.
- Our stomachs are weak because we can't drink water from the streams. We're always carrying those water bottles around.
- We are weak because we have to ride in our cars everywhere instead of walking.
- We are weak because we always have to have someone else carry our loads.
- We are weak because we have trouble sitting on their church benches — often taking chairs to church.
- We are weak because we drive too slowly and slow down for those holes in the road.

- We are weak because we are so fastidious with our bathroom needs, plus we have to have that special soft paper.
- We are weak because we have to take anti-malaria pills — and still get malaria
- Our skin is weak because it burns in the sun.
- We are weak because we can't eat hot pepper.

All these sound reasonable to me. After all, it's all a matter of perspective.

OTHER CULTURAL OBSERVATIONS

On one occasion I angered our Administrator. We were having a *sherehe* (celebration) for the hospital staff, and I announced that we would be starting promptly at 2PM. And we did. I announced that we weren't using "African time" which would have meant starting perhaps by 3PM. This is what offended Bernard. I regretted doing this, for it was a definite cultural faux pas on my part.

There's another aspect of Tanzanians that I can't really explain. They often refer to one of their own as "the white one." The first time I heard this was from Bernard. He holds a Masters Degree and was the most educated Tanzanian I worked with besides the doctors. In reference to a woman on Female Ward he once said, *"It's the white one"*. I knew we had no Caucasians on the ward, so I'm sure I looked a bit quizzical. I found out that this term was generally used to describe someone who "wasn't as black" — somewhat lighter in complexion. I know the term "black" is out in reference to Americans of the African heritage, but very few such Americans are really black. Generally they are shades of brown. Certainly in sub-Saharan Africa the people do indeed approximate the color black. But there are shades even of black. Therefore, the ones who are lesser black or lighter-skinned are referred to as "the white one". If you went to Female Ward and tried to find "the white one", you may come away without a clue. Indeed the Africans are quite attuned to color and can tell the difference. In fact, a young woman with a lighter skin color brings a higher "bride price". Why? I really don't know the answer. I've wondered if it's the influence of the whites who dominated Tanzania for several centuries before their independence — Portuguese, Germans, and then the British. Since they were the leaders and had more money, perhaps Tanzanians saw them as more capable or more intelligent. They might have then transferred some of this thinking to one of their own who was lighter in color. Pure conjecture on my part. This may have nothing to do with the various shades of color. Nevertheless, this color differentiation was something we observed a number of times.

"BURNOUT" — aka "THE BIG B-O"
("EMPTY CUP SYNDROME")

"It is not the critic who counts, not the man who points out how the strong man stumbled or where those who do things could have done them better. The credit belongs to the man who is actually in the arena, whose face is marred by dust and sweat and blood, who strives valiantly, who fails and comes up short again and again. But such a person has great enthusiasm and great devotion and spends himself in a worthy cause. At best he knows the triumph of high achievement. At the worst, if he fails, at least he has while daring greatly. His place shall never be with those cold and timid souls who have failed to try and know neither victory nor defeat."

— Theodore Roosevelt

You probably know that the term 'burnout', as it was first used, had to do with the 'people helping' professions. Your trusty missionary doc certainly was not immune to this malady. Actually the term is now grossly overused, so as to have lost any real meaning. You can be burned out on everything form hot dogs to watching baseball. In fact some people seem to wear the term as some kind of 'badge of honor' — seemingly bragging about it. But I can assure you that those of us in the people helping professions are often quite late in realizing that we are victims of B.O. As a result, we'll often deny the fact. Then if or when we realize it, we feel guilty and are embarrassed — as if we are somehow weak and have succumbed to some irretrievable disorder. We feel like a failure. None of these feelings are true, and none of us are immune. (Even Jesus the Great Physician needed times of solitude and rest). Also B.O. fools us by coming on slowly and insidiously; consequently, we don't understand our feelings.

<u>What causes burnout?:</u> Over work; too much stress and decision making over too long a time; simple physical fatigue and sleep deprivation accelerate its onset; too much sorrow and sadness experienced; disappointment in people or situations.

What about depression causing burnout? Rather than depression being a cause of burnout; it's the other way around. Burnout can result in depression; so depression becomes a symptom of B.O.

My own slide toward burnout was the direct result of all the above listed causes. It was finally precipitated by a period of time when I was the only doctor at Chimala Mission Hospital for five consecutive months. This meant I was <u>on call all the time</u> — 24/7 for 150 days — seeing all the hospitalized patients in our 89 bed hospital, doing all the emergency surgery, doing all the difficult obstetrical deliveries, performing all the Caesarean sections. At that time we were having about 120 deliveries per month with about 20 C-sections per month. WHEW! Makes me tired all over again just thinking about it. From the above you can see that just the overwhelming work was very physically challenging. Add to this the often quite difficult decision making; the ever present expectancy of being called — day or night; the all too common horrible pain, suffering, and death; and the anxiety of either <u>not knowing what is wrong or knowing but not having the capability to act on it.</u>

Tired yet!? Me too. It's painful thinking back on that time. I was at the point of just robotically going through the motions. I found no joy in what I was doing. In fact, I found no joy in anything. I found out that a short time away (even 1-2 days) really did nothing to help. My personal notes at times were so heavily laden with terribly depressive statements that it's frankly quite embarrassing to read them — much less share them. I even documented that I was hesitant to go to sleep at night, for I would face the same thing the next morning. A high point each day was checking off the previous day on my calendar. Isn't that awful! The main thing I looked forward to about five days each week was my ten mile bike ride. For at least this short period of time, I was away (no phones or 'beepers'). I was basically unreachable as I vigorously pedaled away. It was great physical exercise, but more than that was the mental release it served.

Following are some thoughts I wrote in 1996 regarding the way I felt at the time:

"I seem detached, uncaring; it all seems so futile. Am I doing any good? What's the use? What difference does it make? Have I lost my compassion, my perspective? Am I capable of caring anymore? I've seen so much pain, suffering, and death. No one knows whether I am doing right or wrong — whether I'm doing my best or not. I worry whether I will allow all this to let me slip — to not do the best I can and consequently, someone will suffer for it."

You can see from this that I was suffering emotionally, but I was "it" — there was no other doctor. I had no recourse. I just had to endure and pray to continue and do the very best I could. Did I survive this period? Yes, I did — first through Lou Ann's understanding. She put up with my moods, my lack of a sense of humor, my lack of spontaneity, etc. I relied on repeated prayer, through my bike riding, through my God-given dogged stubbornness. Inwardly I had come to grips with my being in the throes of burn-out. As I mentioned, I totally thought this was my failure and mentioned it to no one. I managed to make it to my next furlough. Another necessary help was our finally hiring another doctor — at my insistence to our Mission Administrator. Dr. Safina left a lot to be desired as a doctor, but at least he was able to take call and do his share of the work. This took a much needed burden off me.

This isn't the end of the story. For those of you who think that burnout is the end of the road — a position from which you can never return, I have some good news. Burnout is not forever; it is not terminal; there is life after burnout; you can recover. It is <u>NOT</u> like one of the early analogies that compared human burnout to a rocket stage that burned all its fuel. This analogy has the concept of being finished or used up. Unlike the rocket stage, you can regenerate — you can recover and function normally again. My happy ending is that I did recover — but not without some scars. What scars? What have I learned? First of all is the knowledge that this can happen to me. Yes, I still look upon it as somewhat of a personal weakness. But that's ok; I learned from it. It can recur. We can choose not to put ourselves in the same position again that led to B.O. Or we can learn to watch for the premonitory symptoms and take steps to change — to stop — to do whatever is necessary to prevent the slide into burnout. I also think that it may easier to reach the point of B.O. once you've been there before. An analogy that fits is that once you've had frostbite, it becomes much easier to have it again — with perhaps less severe conditions. And so it is with burnout.

I also realized that you can have B.O. in one area but not others. Just because I might be burned out as a physician or a tennis player does not mean I'm burned out in all areas. So B.O. is preferential — or you could say, limited to certain areas.

ATTITUDE; ATTITUDE; ATTITUDE: This certainly isn't the answer to all situations; but it's an important aspect in dealing with, recovering from, and even overcoming Burn-Out.

Attitude determines how we do anything — anything, whether great or small. And yes, we are in charge of our attitudes — the way we feel. And we can change attitudes and feelings. Feelings are not in control. Feelings can be changed. A definite truism is that you can act your way into feeling. I totally believe this! Let me share a personal example. Earlier in my life I tended to be grumpy and downright irritable in the early morning. I explained it away, much as you might, by saying, *"I'm not a morning person."* Poor excuse. Somewhere along the line I decided to change my morning behavior and "acted my way into feeling." It worked! When I went to work one morning at 6AM, I forced myself to smile and say, "Good morning", and to talk to people. One of the biggest compliments I've received was from a nurse one morning. She said, *"I'm glad you're on; you're always so cheerful in the morning."* Wow! She didn't know how much I appreciated that.

Was this fake behavior? No. Oh well, maybe so at the beginning; but later it became a real habit pattern — the way I should have been all along.

<u>Quotations:</u> It's quite obvious that I like quotations; quotations that show wisdom and consequently inspire. They helped me, and I frequently read them. I referred to them even more as I struggled with B.O. Here are some quotes that I have used:

"Lord, I claim victory right now over the giant/s of _____ (these are anything that keeps you from being the person you know you should be). I recognize that the giant/s are coming against the Christian example I should show. Just as You defeated giants when you walked on this earth, You can defeat them through me now; for You are my life. I trust You to produce peace and self-control through me. I cannot handle what is to come or what is already here. But You can. Respond through me when the pressure comes. Remind me that the battle is Yours."

- Anonymous

Part of a quote from missionary Hudson Taylor:

"I would begin the day with prayer, determined not to take my eye of Him for a moment. But pressure of duties, sometimes very trying, and constant interruptions apt to be so wearing, caused me to forget Him. Then one's nerves get so fretted in this climate that temptations to irritability, hard thoughts and sometimes unkind words are all the more difficult to control."

A quote from Dr. Thomas Hale (long-term medical missionary in Nepal) sums up the dilemma I felt too often as a Christian missionary physician:

"Not all of the cases we see are dramatic. Most of our time is spent in treating the large numbers of patients who are not so seriously ill and who do not readily engage our sympathy. It is when we deal with these patients — frequently neurotic, querulous, impatient, insistent, and unappreciative — that we realize how truly deficient we are in the love of Christ, without which our ministry of medicine is but an empty shell."

FOSTERING DEPENDENCY?

"If we work on marble, it will perish. If we work on brass, time will efface it.
If we rear temples, time will crumble them into dust. But if we work on
immortal minds, if we imbue them with principles with the just fear of
God and love of our fellow men, we engrave on those tablets something
which will brighten all eternity."

– Daniel Webster

My experiences and thoughts on dependency come from both sides of the 'pond' — from working in an inner city ER to the bush country of Tanzania. It's a phenomenon of people. Period. It's not related to race, location, wealth, religion, or status. Inside all of us potentially lies a dependent person who feels entitled. The following thoughts can apply anywhere, even though they're mostly based on our African experiences:

"But we have so much and they have so little; shouldn't we help them?"
"I'm being selfish if I keep it all for myself."
"We just need to get them started."

These and other similar cries need to be seriously reconsidered. As Christians, we should have a God-given desire to help those who are less fortunate than we are. However, at the inner core of mankind there is also this built in desire to have what others have. Even more than this seems to be the desire to get these things as easily as possible. Another truism is that people expect something to continue once it's started (the inertia factor). So we quickly grow to depend on things or money given to us. And what's more; if something is withdrawn, then it's felt that *'something that was rightfully mine'* was taken away. The vicious cycle of dependency is at work.

I've just summarized the very heart of what we in the USA call the "welfare mentality" — aka the "dependency syndrome." Some also refer to this as the "debility of dependency" (crippling effect). Many well meaning missionaries and humanitarian organizations have surreptitiously contributed to the siren song of dependency.

The dependency on money or things coming from outside sources is inexorably more difficult to stop or reverse than it is to prevent — like stopping a rushing stream or an avalanche. Once begun; it develops a 'life of its own.' You can easily become the 'bad guy' if you try to change the process. Many very sincere and dedicated individuals and agencies have tried and failed to reverse the dependency syndrome. The answer is prevention — prevention — prevention!

"Ownership fosters stewardship." This is another truism of mankind. People simply must have a stake in something themselves (ownership). It must cost them something — time, work, goods, management, money. Then they can take pride in and responsibility for whatever the equipment, project, or activity.

Let me give a couple of examples that I experienced:

1) When I first began serving at Chimala, I discovered that an inordinately large percentage (20-25%) of our clinic visits was comprised of mission workers and their dependents. A dependent was defined as someone who lived in the house of the worker. It did not include adult children, but knowing the size of Tanzanian families, the number probably averaged 6-8 per worker (perhaps a total of 600-700 people). This group received free clinic visits including any tests or medicines. We served a population in excess of 12,000 in our area. You can do the math and readily recognize the disproportionate numbers.

I realized that our system was being abused by our workers and families — having too many visits for minor problems and getting too many free medicines. I suspected that some of our patients gave away or sold these medicines. I initiated a new policy that required each patient to pay a small amount — much less than the usual fees. This way they still received good benefits but had some "ownership" in their care. It is often true that if people pay nothing, they think little of what is received — even health care.

I made it clear that the money collected went into a fund that was to be supervised by the local church. It was to be used for widows and needy families.

In the very first month the percentage of visits by workers and their families dropped to 10% (down from the 20-25%). Amazing results in my experiment on how to combat the "dependency syndrome". Of course I caught some flak regarding my decision, but I strongly think it was the right course to follow.

2) This example is about a Tanzanian church that was built with donated funds. It was stated many times to the church leaders that the money was a gift. After the church was completed, any future expenses or repairs were their responsibility. You're ahead of me! When a tree fell on the roof and caused damage, the church leaders came wanting money to fix the roof. Why? The reasoning was that the church belonged to those who gave the money to build it. And since this was the case, it was their responsibility to repair it. (The church leaders obviously didn't grasp the import of the original agreement. Or did they?).

I again reiterate that I'm not 'picking on' the Tanzanians. As I've said, it's people. Yes, even you and me. This syndrome is extremely contagious and resistant to cure.

THOUGHTS / CAUTIONS REGARDING DEPENDENCY

- Don't give a 'knee jerk' response to requests. Give liberally, yet cautiously, and only after deliberation and consideration. Ask local missionaries and others who know about the matter. Ask them about the need, those requesting help, and any possible ramifications. Most important!

- You will be simply amazed at the infinite variety of requests for support — simply endless. The key again is to check out all requests as completely as possible.
- In our experience in Africa, we discovered that if we said, *"I'll think about it"* or *"Maybe we can do that"*, it was heard as a *"YES"*. If we decided not to help after having used these phrases, we would be told, *"But you promised."* I know in our culture these terms are a *"polite no"*, but they are a *"Yes"* in their culture. We had to alter our words to something like, *"I cannot give you an answer now"* or *"That is not something I can do."*
- It is harder for you to say "No", than it is for them to accept "No".
- Resist — resist <u>ongoing</u> support. To give a one time gift or support is one thing, but to agree to any long-term commitment is quite another. You must make it quite clear from the beginning that you are giving a one-time gift. You can always change this arrangement later if you deem necessary. When we lived in Africa, my wife and I would put these matters in writing and have the people sign. This is especially important if you agree to some long-term support. By all means stick to the agreement. Make it clear whether it is a gift (not to be repaid) or a loan (with terms of repayment).
- Once you give either a one-time gift or for ongoing support, you must get ready for the onslaught. What am I talking about? I'm talking about the onslaught of very plausible reasons you'll be given as to why you should either give more or give again — and again — and again. You will also have requests from other people — word spreads.
- A caution as to following up your support: No matter how seemingly well intentioned the recipient is about your following up, you will find that it becomes quite laborious if not down right impossible to do so. But do it anyway.
- Receiving external support over a long period weakens the national. First of all it takes away their allegiance to their own people. Their allegiance is to YOU. You would be amazed at

how much energy and time they spend on this. It also decreases their initiative.

- Locally it becomes a 'status thing' to receive support from the United States. Then you have the predictable result — jealousy. You wind up with two camps — the ones who get support and the ones who don't.

- Another strange quirk of human nature is that it can grow to "bite the hand that feeds it." I am saying that you will be made to feel like the bad guy if you don't give more or if you decrease or stop your support.

- You can never be sure how much support someone gets from other sources. This is another reason to check with other locals who know the person and the situation.

- It is another general human truism that something free is not worth much. *"If it doesn't cost me anything, it must not be worth much."* I've seen this to be true of medical care. This is why I am opposed to free clinics. Oftentimes people come to these clinics in order to get medicine for later use or to sell. They should pay something — no matter how small.

There is much written about the vicious cycle of dependency in missionary articles. I implore you to be a part of the solution — not a part of the problem. There are other alternatives — other ways to help. Be an enabler, a teacher. There are many ministries that emphasize "tent making". This has to do with teaching various skills or trades.

Please consider the things that I've said. I hope that I didn't sound too negative or cynical. What I said comes from the experience of living in Africa for six years (and other experiences). Of course you will make mistakes and get "stung". It has happened to me more than once. Just learn from your mistakes and prayerfully keep trying and helping.

COMPARISON OF DELIVERY ROOMS

"Technology is a way of multiplying the unnecessary."

I've written a lot about OB but not so much about the Delivery Room itself. First of all we had only one room for our some 120 deliveries per month. Our room had three "delivery beds" and because of our volume it was rather common to have all beds filled with women in active labor. Our room was about 10X25 feet. That's right; about like a good sized pantry or closet in the USA. The beds were flat (no adjustments) with a thin foam rubber pad covered with a thick plastic material. We eventually did get what were billed as delivery beds (they would "break down" at their mid point which allowed women to get in stirrups for delivery), but our mid-wives still preferred to just use them as flat beds. We did have a rolling screen available that could be used between the beds for "privacy". This was hardly ever used. There was an overhead crooked and creaky fan that operated when we had electricity. This only served to spread the heat and odor around. Running water (directly from the river) was available in the room. There were windows to the outside, but they were positioned high enough so as to prevent any peering. I should also say that the bedroom windows in our house were only about 100 yards from these windows. How often we were awakened by the "sounds of OB" — the cries of pain!

The hours I spent in this room defy calculation. Waiting, watching, listening to fetal heart beats, waiting some more, sweating, or laboring myself with a difficult delivery. Just imagine the stifling heat mixed with the sounds and the smells of sweat and blood and amniotic fluid. Yes, it was enough to make you nauseated; but fortunately I never had trouble with this — a blessing.

This OB area was a room of great joy and of great sadness. I felt so sad for the mothers whose babies had died. This was especially true because right next to their bed might be a mother with a healthy, crying baby. Who knows what was going through the minds of these sad mothers? Upon observing them, they usually showed no emotion — just flat, resolute faces with a blank stare. It was their culture's way of dealing with tragedy. We would move these mothers to another area as quickly as possible.

Despite our setting we had excellent OB results. This was because of attentiveness during labor. Our nurse mid-wives handled the routine deliveries and called me if there was a problem. Boy, is this ever understated! We saw basically every possible OB complication and then some. This was because of our volume and because many women were referred to us who were already in trouble — referred from their villages by a local lady who did deliveries. Often the referrals would be too late — the baby would have been in distress too long to survive. We performed C-sections only when the life of the mother or baby was in jeopardy — not for convenience sake or any other reason. Our C-section rate ran consistently right at 10%. Remember that some of our women were "referred" because they were having difficulty. This made our percentage as high as it was. (Compare this with your local hospital.)

We had the blessing of being present for the birth of one of our grandchildren shortly after this time. Her birth was in Indianapolis at St. Francis Hospital. The contrast between what I've described at Chimala and our daughter's labor room is drastic and almost beyond description. So I'm going to list the things that were present in the USA and NOT present in Chimala. I am not doing this to denigrate Chimala or to heap praise on the USA. My point is to again show the stark contrasts between our world and that of a Third World or developing country rural hospital.

ST. Francis Delivery Room:

- Room larger and only one bed for delivery [no congestion]
- Storage cabinets (4)
- Automatic B.P. machine

- Fetal monitor
- Central monitoring screen
- Computer terminal
- Two IV pumps
- Baby warmer
- Surgical light
- All needed delivery supplies and equipment
- Intercom system
- Telephone
- Television and VCR player
- Call button
- Obstetrical bed with infinite electrical adjustments and positions
- Private bathroom
- Recliner chair
- Table (for reading, eating, etc.)
- Two other chairs for guests, etc.
- Lotion dispenser
- Sink complete with soap and towels
- Four trash cans
- Ultrasound equipment
- Thermostat with automatic heating and cooling capability
- Wall mounted Oxygen and suction
- Smoke alarm
- Sprinkler system
- Pictures on wall
- Baby trolley for transport
- Doors to room

The above list includes visible, tangible items. The following are not tangible but were present at St. Francis and are equally important:

- Humidity Control
- Odor (pleasant)
- Cleanliness

- Organization
- Efficiency
- Quiet (one patient per room)

This comparison is so vivid; for Lou Ann and I witnessed the birth of our granddaughter, Hope Faidley, in the St. Francis Hospital not long after our return from Tanzania. By the way, we also missed the birth of two other grandchildren (Alexander and Hannah Faidley) when we were in Tanzania. Kind of difficult on us grandparents.

"YOU KNOW YOU'VE BEEN IN AFRICA
TOO LONG WHEN............."

*"Nothing touches me that has not passed through the hands of my Father.
Nothing. Everything I experience is designed to prepare me
for serving others more effectively. Everything."*

This chapter represents another of our ongoing themes when we lived in Africa. These are humorous to us (and back home), but are things we'd never share with our Tanzanian friends. Culture stress being an ongoing phenomenon, these vignettes were concocted and served as another coping mechanism. Over time I kept a record of anecdotes or occurrences that depicted this short section's theme. I would pluck them out and use them at strategic points in my Newsletters or when giving talks in the USA. If our Tanzanian friends could spend time in the USA, I'm sure they could just as easily accumulate a list in answer to, "You know you've been in the USA too long when _____."

I would like to say here that you can never become totally "African" — never become absolutely immersed in their culture, so that the local people look upon you as one of their own. When a missionary tries to do this, we say they are trying to "go African." It is really intended as kind of a derogatory comment. Some few do come close to total cultural assimilation, but it's only the very few.

Generally if an American missionary tries to "go African" ("go native"), for the most part they will never last. What do I mean? To live like, eat like, move about like, and work like the African usually would bring a host of ongoing problems and illnesses. Very easily I can show an immediate problem with "going native" by a couple examples. One would simply have to do with drinking the water Africans drink. Raging diarrhea would soon occur. Our gastrointestinal systems are just not used to the bacterial load in their water. Another easy example would be malaria. Whatever 'natural or acquired immunity' the Africans have toward malaria would be totally lacking in newcomer missionaries. In short, missionaries should not be too cavalier about illness and dangers. They should not be dismissive of proper preventive medicine. Treat the water and take anti-malarial medicine!

There's another reason missionaries cannot fully "go native". Africans know that missionaries have the capability of returning to the USA should it really be necessary. They have seen this too many times. Missionaries with good intentions of not leaving have done so because of severe illness, death in their family, or some other urgent situation. The bottom line is that Africans DO NOT EXPECT us to "go native." In fact, I think they find it a bit strange. It does not hurt our influence if we don't attempt it. It is not a sign of weakness or a sign of not helping enough if missionaries <u>don't</u> try to "go native."

Here's the list we concocted over the years:

"You've been in Africa too long when……..":

- You hear me saying, "Oh, the two new cases are only anthrax and tetanus."
- The goat walking down the aisle at church hardly gets your attention.
- I hear Lou Ann say, "What odor? I don't smell anything."
- You don't bother to brush the flies away from your food.
- We cannot remember the English word for something.
- The bare breast is hardly noticed.
- I find myself getting excited over a box of rather stale Kellogg's cornflakes we found in the market.
- I find myself not getting excited over killing another cobra on our front walkway.
- Lou Ann is talking in her sleep —— in Swahili!!
- The following note from a patient's chart doesn't seem unusual: "Patient arrived unconscious — dumped from the Iringa bus."

- Hot Cokes taste good.
- I think every fever is from malaria and every belly pain is from worms.
- Someone says, "Oh, that's just another giraffe crossing the road."
- You see nothing uncouth anymore about "nose picking" in public.
- The elongated, stretched, hole-laden Masaii ears are looking kind of attractive.
- I am heard saying, "What are you taking about, this is a good road."
- We are beginning to agree with the Tanzanian philosophy of "labda kesho." (perhaps it'll happen tomorrow)
- A flying critter across my operative field hardly gains my attention.
- We've come to realize that Americans drive on the wrong side of the road. (In Tanzania we drive "British style" — on the left side)
- McDonalds; Thanksgiving; Labor Day; the Yankees; what are these?
- "But doesn't everyone have the "Big D" (diarrhea) off and on?"
- We see someone overweight and know that they are healthy and have money. (This is what Africans think about any person who is overweight — whether one of their own or an ex-patriot.)

* And the list can go on and on and ………

FIRST DAY BACK

"To whom little is not enough, nothing is enough."

— Greek quotation

People always ask me, *"What's it like in Africa?"* In this chapter I'll let some contrasts answer the question. After these I think it'll be more than obvious.

The following are some comparisons between my experiences at our "bush" hospital in Chimala and my first day back in the ER in the USA. (Fayette Memorial Hospital in Connersville, IN):

USA	TANZANIA
• One hour drive each way to the hospital	* Two minute walk to hospital
• Thirteen bed ER	* No ER
• Insurance, Medicaid, Third Party payers	* None
• Occasional black patient	* All patients are black
• Everyone speaks English	* Rare English speaker
• First case was heart attack	* No heart attack in 5 years
• Dictated all ER charts	* All charts handwritten
• Talked to many referral doctors on telephone	* No telephone

• No malaria cases	* Malaria: most common disease
• No HIV/AIDS cases	* Many HIV/AIDS cases (see Chapter on HIV/AIDS)
• Ambulances / Paramedics	* No ambulances /paramedics
• Sink and monitors in every room	* One sink and no monitor On 20 bed ward
• One patient per room	* 20 patients per ward (one room)
• EKG's, electrolytes, blood gases, kidney function tests, etc.	* None available
• Many elderly and Nursing Home patients	* Average life expectancy 51 (No Nursing Homes)
• Receiving Fax or computer copy of patients' records	* What? *You've got to be kidding!"*
• Many smokers	* Virtually no smokers
• Minimal acuity cases — many early presentations of minor problems	* High acuity of cases - late presentations
• Comparatively few patients	* Usually inundated with patients
• Bathrooms everywhere with flush toilets	* One bathroom per ward with several <u>*holes in the floor*</u>

- Oxygen in every room * One oxygen tank for the entire hospital

- CT scans and MRI * Perhaps one in the entire country

- Efficiency by all staff * See Chapter on *"Efficiency"*

Actually my list only begins to show the differences in our "bush hospital" and the ones you know. I think by now you very clearly get the picture. You might be thinking, *"How can you help anyone in that setting?"* As I've tried to show in other chapters, much good can be done for most people with what we had available. I do hasten to add that we had as much capability at Chimala as other comparable hospitals in Tanzania. Actually we were among one of the better ones — not the other way around. Believe me; it's true! We had much better statistics in some very critical areas than did our referral government hospital in Mbeya — one hour drive away.

Let me tell you about two areas that elucidate the good care we gave at Chimala. This doesn't fit into my "First Day Back" list, but it shows that we were able to give very good care. These two areas are rarely encountered in the USA — certainly the malaria example. First I'll focus on falciparum malaria. This is the most serious of the several types of malaria and the one most common at Chimala. It has been called "blackwater fever" over the years. That's because of how it affects the blood and the kidneys, resulting in hemoglobinuria — or very dark brown/black urine (from the breakdown of blood). It also commonly affects the brain — resulting in what is called cerebral malaria with seizures, coma, and potential death. Most textbooks tell of about 20% mortality rate in cerebral malaria — even with treatment. At Chimala our mortality rate in cerebral malaria was in the range of 10%. We were quite proud of our results. They were the result of much time, follow-up, and attention to details.

My other example is something of which I'm even more proud. It's the medical condition that is called ECLAMPSIA. This is a serious (potentially fatal) condition in pregnant women around the time of labor and delivery (see chapter on "Obstetrics"). It is manifested by severe hypertension (high blood pressure), edema, and seizures. It's an entity of unknown cause that most frequently occurs with the first pregnancy. However, it doesn't have to follow this pattern. It's a true medical emergency! The objective of treatment is to treat the hypertension and the seizures and then to have the women deliver as soon as possible — whether vaginally or by C-section. We usually had perhaps one such case per month. In the five years I was at Chimala we had NO maternal deaths from eclampsia. I found out that on one weekend at our Government Referral Hospital they had three deaths from eclampsia. How could this be you may be thinking. I can easily tell you; and no, I'm not bragging. It has to do with proper medical knowledge, a supply of the proper medicines, spending the time ("staying on top of the case"), and delivering the patient in a timely manner. Once when a Government Review Team came to Chimala, they didn't believe that we had no eclampsia deaths. They wanted to review our records and charts. I was never more happy to comply with a Review Team — whether at Chimala or in the USA. It made our results even more gratifying to know that they knew of our successful treatment of eclampsia.

REFLECTIONS

*"If I speak fluently the languages of all African tribes and am endowed with ulti-
mate cultural sensitivity; but have no love, I am only a relentless banging drum
and my missionary service is meaningless.*

*If I have the gift of healing and can successfully treat any tropical disease
and deliver the most difficult OB case; but do not have compassion, the Spirit of
God is not living in me. I am nothing.*

*If I have the gift of teaching medicine and healthcare beyond that of Albert
Schweitzer, but do not tell the story of Jesus, I have wasted my talents as well as
my words.*

*If I spend forty years in a foreign land and die of a tropical disease; but do
not walk unselfishly with God while lovingly teaching His message, my ultimate
value to the people and to my Lord is void.*

*And now these four remain; language learning, cultural sensitivity, healing,
and love. But the greatest of these is love."*

– Janice Bingham
(This rendition by Janice probably looks familiar to most of you.
It's based on I Corinthians Chapter 13.)

During our last year at Chimala (1997) we tried to obtain the
services of another physician who would qualify as the
Mganga Mkuu (Chief Doctor). We were able to hire a Tanzanian doctor, but he lacked the ability to serve in this capacity. As a missionary
hospital, we just weren't able to pay what was needed to acquire the
services of a better trained or experienced Tanzanian physician. Consequently, it didn't take a prophet to think that the hospital would
decline in its quality of service when we left (Lou Ann, Janice, and
yours truly). Jokingly I said that, *"The hospital would begin to decline as
soon as the diesel fumes dissipated upon our departure."* It's true that some
things declined, but for the most part the hospital has sustained a
good quality of care for such a location.

We kept up with the hospital as best we could during the ensuing years. We returned on short-term trips (4-5 weeks) five different times, and I served in whatever capacity was needed. Our last visit was in 2015 (hope to return in 2018). Of course we could see things that needed to be changed, but this isn't possible unless you remain on the scene. I want to emphasize that being present is vital in order to effect and sustain change and improvement.

It's difficult for the physicians at Chimala to have total allegiance to the hospital. Part of this is due to the country's policy that allows doctors to have their own clinics — separate and apart from their main work. You can see that this could lead to a problem of divided loyalty. The nursing service is limited because the Chimala administrators weren't able to pay what the government paid at their hospitals and clinics. Consequently, it's difficult to get nurses; and if they came to Chimala, they often would depart when they got a government job. I can just say that patient care suffered because of these and other situations.

You can see the difficulty for Lou Ann and me when we returned. We love the place and the people so much. We just wanted the hospital to improve its services more quickly. And yet we knew it was not possible for us to do from afar. We maintain a pride in the hospital and brag to others about it. We talk about Chimala and tell "African stories" any time possible (maybe too much at times). When I went back to work in the ER, the staff loved it when I told "African stories." It's indelibly part of us — our African time of service. We wouldn't swap it for anything.

In my ongoing effort to define "What is Third World?", there is one constant. That being, THINGS CHANGE SLOWLY. In today's world this is especially detrimental. It means that people or country's get further and further behind. This was manifested upon our first return trip to Chimala after being away for eight years (1997 — 2005). Very little had changed.

I wonder if you can guess the one major change that had occurred. It was the cell phone! It seemed that virtually everyone had a cell phone. Even Masaii ladies that came in from the far 'bush' would have a cell phone in a pouch hanging from their neck. Now why they needed them or whom they talked to — that's a different story.

The other area that had changed regarded HIV/AIDS. (see Chapter on "HIV/AIDS"). We found quite adequate anti-viral medicines available and a Clinic to treat the patients' problems. What a drastic change from our years! If you remember, we had no anti-viral medicines during our tenure. Thanks to the Gates Foundation and the Government of Tanzania for this tremendous service. This was all free for the patients. (Unfortunately, there was an increase in the incidence of HIV/AIDS.)

It has been the highlight of my medical career to deliver care where it's needed the most — and to serve in the name of Christianity. Lou Ann frequently tells people that it was the most needed and useful that she'd ever felt. As I implied in the "Introduction", this is a reason for my delay and hesitation in finishing the book — how to significantly portray our lives and its monumental meaning to us in written form. I've tried. There is so much more............

I want to encourage all health care workers to consider giving of their skills and time in service to those most in need of medical care. Quite often this is in a developing country. After you go the first time, you'll be "hooked". You'll want to continue — and to take others with you. Express your compassion. GO AND SERVE !

"As we have been given the gifts of healing, what better role for us as deliverers of health care than to be the ones to bring healing to those left frightened and alone; crying for the sickness and loss of their fathers, mothers, brothers, sisters, children, friends, and yes, even enemies. The only way we can truly heal the broken-hearted is to seek the cure and accept it by faith. Jesus is the cure and the answer for the world's pain today, tomorrow, and every tomorrow to come."

— Dr.Joule O'Connor

CPSIA information can be obtained
at www.ICGtesting.com
Printed in the USA
LVOW07s2009010118

561456LV00001B/125/P

9 781457 559518